Declarations of Dependence

SERIES EDITORS · *Marco Abel and Roland Végső*

PROV
OCAT
IONS

Something in the world forces us to think.
—Gilles Deleuze

The world provokes thought. Thinking is nothing but the human response to this provocation. Thus the very nature of thought is to be the product of a provocation. This is why a genuine act of provocation cannot be the empty rhetorical gesture of the contrarian. It must be an experimental response to the historical necessity to act. Unlike the contrarian, we refuse to reduce provocation to a passive noun or a state of being. We believe that real moments of provocation are constituted by a series of actions that are best defined by verbs or even infinitives—verbs in a modality of potentiality, of the promise of action. To provoke is to intervene in the present by invoking an as yet undecided future radically different from what is declared to be possible in the present and, in so doing, to arouse the desire for bringing about change. By publishing short books from multiple disciplinary perspectives that are closer to the genres of the manifesto, the polemical essay, the intervention, and the pamphlet than to traditional scholarly monographs, "Provocations" hopes to serve as a forum for the kind of theoretical experimentation that we consider to be the very essence of thought.

www.provocationsbooks.com

Declarations of Dependence

Money, Aesthetics, and the Politics of Care

SCOTT FERGUSON

UNIVERSITY OF NEBRASKA PRESS · LINCOLN AND LONDON

Portions of the introduction were originally
published on the *Critical Inquiry* blog, *In the
Moment*, as "Bond, Treasury Bond: 007 Is Out
of Cash, but Your Government Can't Be."

The series editors would like to thank
Jon Carter, Anne Johnson, Robert
Lipscomb, and Dillon Rockrohr for
their work on the manuscript.

Library of Congress
Cataloging-in-Publication Data
Names: Ferguson, Scott (Assistant
Professor), author.
Title: Declarations of dependence:
money, aesthetics, and the politics
of care / Scott Ferguson.
Description: Lincoln: University of Nebraska
Press, 2018. | Series: Provocations
Identifiers: LCCN 2017044659
ISBN 9781496201928 (paper: alk. paper)
ISBN 9781496207104 (epub)
ISBN 9781496207111 (mobi)
ISBN 9781496207128 (pdf)
Subjects: LCSH: Money. | Critical
theory. | Aesthetics.
Classification: LCC HG221 .F433 2018 |
DDC 332.401—dc23 LC record available
at https://lccn.loc.gov/2017044659

Set in Sorts Mill Goudy by E. Cuddy.
Designed by N. Putens.

CONTENTS

ACKNOWLEDGMENTS

I am profoundly grateful to the family, friends, and colleagues who enabled me to write *Declarations of Dependence*. I thank series editors Marco Abel and Roland Végső for their guidance in shepherding an unlikely project to completion; Brendan Cook for his indefatigable support and command of early modern metaphysics and aesthetics; friends William Saas, Todd Barnes, and Jonathan Haynes for providing judicious feedback on imperfect chapters; and Steven Shaviro for his stunning magnanimity in responding to my manuscript. For both financial and professional support, my thanks to Warren Mosler; the Binzagr Institute for Sustainable Prosperity (especially Fadhel Kaboub and Mathew Forstater); the Modern Money Network; Roland Greene, Luis Rincon, and Adam Morris at *Arcade*; Jordan Rose and the History of Art Department at UC Berkeley; and my associates in the Department of Humanities and Cultural Studies at the University of South Florida (Dan Belgrad, Andrew Berish, Sara Dykins Callahan, Maria Cizmic, Bill Cummings, James D'Emilio, Benjamin Goldberg, Todd Jurgess, Christie Rinck, and Brook Sadler). This book would have been impossible without the ongoing engagement of my comrades in the MMT community. Most dear to me are Jorge Amar Benet, Raúl Carrillo, Alexander Douglas, Timothy

Fong, David Freund, David Glotzer, Mitch Green, Rohan Grey, Robert Hockett, Stavros Karageorgis, Stephanie Kelton, Mikey McDowell, Rebecca Rojer, Maxximilian Seijo, Nathan Cedric Tankus, Pavlina Tcherneva, and Benjamin Wilson.

I have long depended on the encouragement of my confidants in the humanities, including Nima Bassiri, Gavin Benke, Stephanie Boluk, Mona Bower, Norman Gendelman, Paul Haacke, James Harker, James Hodge, Tung-Hui Hu, Anna Kornbluh, Benjamin Morgan, Julie Napolin, Scott Richmond, Peter Skafish, Yannik Thiem, Heather Warren-Crow, Damon Young, and Genevieve Yue. Living in Florida, I have come to rely on the generosity of Alycia Alexander-Guerra, Sari Altschuler, Jan Awai, Devon Brady, Gena Camoosa, Jennifer Cazenave, Brian Connolly, Jasdeep Cook, Nicholas de Villiers, Darcie Fontaine, Audrey Raymi Grounds, Ross Grounds, Julia Irwin, Chris Parsons, Steve Prince, Mario Rendina, Lois Rendina, Adam Schwartz, and Aaron Walker. Meanwhile, I owe so much to so many in California. Big ups to my Valley Boys: Romesh Fernando, Joseph Gordon-Levitt, Josh Klinghoffer, Brian Smith, and Jason Weissbrod. Thank you to mentors Whitney Davis, Colin Gardner, Ann Haley, Kevin McDermott, Chris Nealon, Anne Nesbet, Constance Penley, Bhaskar Sarkar, Kaja Silverman, Charis Thompson, and Linda Williams.

My family has continuously supported my endeavors—astoundingly, even when no one knows what I am up to. I am forever indebted to my loving and open-minded parents, Frank Ferguson and Lisa Ferguson, and to my sister Lauren Ferguson-Wilhite and her family, Jeff Wilhite, Aidan Wilhite, and Preston Wilhite. I cherish Jeanne Rust, Robert Rust, Paul Rust, Lesley Arfin, Anne Rust, and Alexis Madsen. I am also thankful to Dennis Levitt and Jane Gordon, whose parent-like guidance and leftist library played essential roles in shaping the person I have become.

At last, I dedicate this book to Amy Rust—and to our two boys, Elias and Aubrey. Amy, thanks for your compassion and brilliance. Thank you for two exhausting little firecrackers. And *thank God* for wine, TV, and grownup conversation. You are my everything.

PROVOCATIONS

Human being is born and remains dependent, yet everywhere she is abandoned. Today, so many yearn to be free from the governing center, but they are more reliant upon its care than they know. Traditionally, critique has answered care's entanglements by insisting that money enslaves and the aesthetic saves. Yet neoliberal fecklessness has revealed the impotence of this dialectic, requiring us to set the historical relation between money and aesthetics on more capacious foundations. For this, critical theory must desert the Marxist image of money as a private, finite, and alienable quantum of value. Instead, it should embrace the heterodoxy of Modern Monetary Theory, for which money is a boundless public center that can be made to support all.

Seize the money relation!
Enlist the aesthetic in money's expansion!
Hail money as the center of caretaking!
Declare your dependence on care's center!
Relinquish attachments to thisness!
Imagine a boundless public center!
Never forsake abstraction for gravity's attractions!
Exalt abstraction as the locus of care!

Introduction

Critique after Modern Monetary Theory

Assume man *to be* man *and his relationship to the world to be a human one: then you can exchange love only for love, trust for trust, etc. If you want to enjoy art, you must be an artistically cultivated person; if you want to exercise influence over other people, you must be a person with a stimulating and encouraging effect on other people. Every one of your relations to man and to nature must be a* specific expression, *corresponding to the object of your will, of your* real individual *life. If you love without evoking love in return—that is, if your loving as loving does not produce reciprocal love; if through a* living expression *of yourself as a loving person you do not make yourself a* beloved one, *then your love is impotent—a misfortune.*
—Karl Marx

Money is no object.
—Stephanie Kelton

In the James Bond film *Spectre* (2015) a cabal of digital surveillance capitalists cum global terrorists attempt to take over the British national intelligence service. This clandestine group builds a flashy high-tech skyscraper in the heart of London, and at one point it is explained that only private investors would be able to afford this cutting-edge structure. In reality the scenes inside the fictitious data center were shot within London's current City Hall. Yet according to the film's harrowing story world, the British government simply does not have the money to commission such an extravagant edifice. Though mentioned only in passing, this comment about the insufficiency of public funds appears to structure the film's entire plot. The story pits what is essentially an embattled government program against the allegedly greater powers of global information capital, imagined as an unruly field of spectral agents that no state can capture or contain. Deemed "Bond for the age of austerity," *Spectre*'s cash-strapped hero still gets a pair of handsome cars as well as a perfectly pressed ensemble for every climate and occasion.[1] Sadly, however, what *Spectre* shows is that today, it is easier to believe a man can single-handedly take down an evil capitalist organization than it is to imagine a government being able to afford dazzling public infrastructures.

Meanwhile, the true specter haunting the latest installment of the Bond franchise is not global info capitalism, as the film's narrative suggests. Rather, it is the limitless reserve of government treasury bonds that, according the contemporary heterodox school of political economy known as Modern Monetary Theory (MMT), could be immediately deployed to uplift everyone. Modern governments are said to spend by "borrowing" treasury bonds.[2] Yet as MMT economist Scott Fullwiler explains, a sovereign currency-issuing government never needs to borrow, or even tax, before issuing such bonds. "Revenues for bond sales or taxes," as Fullwiler has it, "do not affect the government's operational ability to spend."[3] Lest we forget, writes Fullwiler, it is impossible for a currency-issuing government to run out of a unit that it alone supplies. Additionally, MMT insists that government can always afford to take care of everyone without risking inflationary price rises, so long as public spending remains directed at real resources and unused productive capacities. MMT's startling revelation, then, is that austerity is a cruel fiction, an unnecessary condition that can be instantly reversed. More pointedly, there are no *economic* constraints to government's capacity to address urgent social and environmental crises; *politics* are the sole reason why we, as a public, cannot have what we need.

Thus, in contrast to what the mainstream press alleged during the 2016 primary race, the U.S. government can afford everything former presidential hopeful Bernie Sanders proposed: universal healthcare; free university education; infrastructure repair; first-rate public housing; environmental retrofitting; and low-cost postal banking. But with MMT, we can do Bernie one better. Just ask Stephanie Kelton, a top MMT economist who also served as Sanders's chief economic advisor for his role as the ranking Democrat on the Senate Budget Committee and subsequent presidential bid. In addition to what Sanders had officially proposed, Kelton suggests, we can also create a high-quality public child- and eldercare service; a robust public arts program; and a federally funded yet communally organized public works system, or "job guarantee," that would grant a living-wage job to everyone who wishes to have one.[4] Think of the latter as something akin to a permanent but more inclusive and locally sensitive version of the Works Progress Administration implemented under the Franklin Delano Roosevelt presidency. This program would not only virtually eradicate problems of un- and underemployment. It would also establish just minimum standards for pay and benefits, put the means of production in the hands of workers, and ensure everyone's right to participate meaningfully in shaping our world.

In order to rescue our society from the self-imposed horrors of austerity, we require neither Bond-like bodily prowess nor the computer-simulated collisions that dominate *Spectre*, along with most contemporary action media. After all, money is not physics, as MMT reminds us, nor is it a "bond" that takes the shape of physics. In contrast to the economic orthodoxy's insistence upon grounding money in local private exchanges, MMT argues that money is a creature of government and a public system of accounting and law. Money involves abstract inscriptions and simultaneous coordination between a centralized government and geographically dispersed institutions, not localized movements of alienable matter. With this, MMT makes perceptible what I call *the unheard-of center* of modern life. Precisely because money remains a centralized, abstract, and inalienable relation, MMT concludes, a currency-issuing polity can forever afford to guarantee persons' employment and involvement, access, and care.

Meanwhile, what I shall refer to as the "Liberal" monetary imagination (in contrast to the imaginary of "small *l*" American "liberalism") has hidden this capacious center behind an alienating physics. In a tremendous feat of disavowal, it manages to reduce an acknowledged abstraction to a singular *contract* and then wrap this narrow association around a *contracted* physics. Thus, to lay bare money's boundless center and attain what is desperately needed, contemporary action media's explosive motion will be, at best, a weak ally and, at worst, an unwitting accomplice in a nefarious vanishing act. In place of *Spectre*'s abstract physics, then, we shall require a more mysterious combination of elements that are at once more powerful and less substantial: a renewed critical praxis and a resolutely public capacity to generate money *out of thin air*.

In this book, I aim to initiate and orient such a praxis by regrounding critical theory in the unheard-of center that MMT makes newly perceptible. To do so, I break with the Marxist understanding of money that has historically guided critical theory as well as the treatment of the aesthetic it has conditioned. Like orthodox economics, Marxism treats money as a more or less passive vehicle for material exchanges that are abstractly mediated. As a result, it tends to denounce the money relation as an inherently privative social process and hence as one that is incapable of serving collective well-being. Yet as MMT demonstrates, money is irreducible to a "crystal of value . . . into which the commodity eagerly solidifies" and out of which its abstract husk "dissolves," as Karl Marx artfully put it in *Capital, Volume One*.[5] By insisting upon what might be called money's *mediated immediacy*, while also reducing the state to a revenue-constrained and generally unproductive spender, Marxism's expressly immanent critique of monetary abstraction reifies the very privation it rejects. As a consequence of adopting this ontology of money, I contend, critical theory misperceives political economy's actual conditions of possibility and hamstrings the most revolutionary weapon within reach.

The Marxist reification of monetary privation, in turn, leads critical theorists to adopt an impoverished conception of the aesthetic, which constricts the curative capacities of money and aesthetics alike. As the conventional narrative has it, the modern bourgeoisie first sought refuge from the Liberal money regime by turning to the realm of sensibility, culture, and art that came to be called "the aesthetic."[6] Whereas the Liberal monetary economy was plagued by sensory deprivation, experiential delimitation, and narrow social interests, the aesthetic sphere made room for sensory heterogeneity and repleteness, free play, and yearnings for universal communion. Although the aesthetic project failed to deliver on its mandate, critical theory invested a great deal of thought and hope in its utopian impulses. For some critical theorists, the aesthetic's failed strivings for autonomy became a form of negative illumination, pointing beyond present alienation toward alternative orders. For others, the aesthetic's sensuous and underdetermined communality made for an incipient utopia in the here-and-now. The aesthetic needed only to be generalized and deepened in order positively to overcome political economic alienation. As I shall claim here, however, in placing what Immanuel Kant called the aesthetic's "unbounded expansion" beyond and against monetary mediation, critical theory forecloses money's boundless public center and delimits aesthetic expansion to a contracted field. In a word, it debilitates money and aesthetics alike.

My book, by contrast, joins critical theory's commitments to sensuous immanence with MMT's ontology of money and makes aesthetics newly answerable to political economy. To do so, it will be necessary to rethink the historical relationship between money and the aesthetic in three ways. First, I argue that money alone harbors the capacity to cultivate a full, diverse, and variable collective life. I risk this claim without appealing to orthodox yarns about self-correcting markets or to mutualist dreams about self-supporting associations that are proffered by advocates of cyber and extra-state currencies. Instead, I presume worldly inclinations toward dissolution and aggression. I critique desires to cure these centrifugal impulses with benevolent forms of mediated immediacy, and I affirm money's unrestricted capacity to socialize labor and accommodate myriad social differences.

Second, I contend that the modern problem of the aesthetic is best understood as a historical symptom. It is a response to the metaphysical *thisness*, or *haecceity*, to which the dominant Liberal ontology of money has reduced monetary abstraction. Coined by theologian Duns Scotus during the thirteenth century, *haecceity* (pronounced "hæk-see-ê-tee") is a metaphysical principle that denies causal dependencies between spatially separated beings. Instead, haecceity contracts the totality of being into the thisness of individuated particulars and, more significant, into the thisness of the contiguous and, typically, material relations that condition individuation. Haecceity eventually becomes the metaphysical basis for the hegemonic

Liberal money form. Shrinking an expansive and noncontiguous social bond into a contracted and alienable relation, the modern Liberal imagination comes to treat monetary abstraction as a kind of *haecceity-in-motion*: a mobile and distinctly decentered thisness that seems to fill and evacuate private and public coffers. When the Liberal money form's contracted dynamics fail to support the social totality, the aesthetic arises as a symptomatic answer to money's haecceity. Specifically, the aesthetic seeks to redeem haecceity's universalizing promise in an alternative and improved form. In place of Liberal money's impoverished thisness, it offers a rich and open haecceity that is supposed to support the social order in a manner that money apparently cannot. Yet the aesthetic project persistently falls short of its aim. This is not merely a consequence of ongoing social domination. It does not owe to the fact that money has somehow penetrated too deeply into social life. It is because haecceity remains an impoverished metaphysical foundation for any social order, no matter how expansive or universal its aims. The aesthetic is a symptom, then, because despite its salutary openings, it ultimately expresses rather than contests the Liberal money form's metaphysical commitment to haecceity. As symptom, the aesthetic participates in making undetectable the nonlocal connections between spatially distant persons and environs that money's public center regularly maintains. It also disguises that center's limitless capacity to overcome neoliberal devastation.

Third, I turn the aesthetic's salutary openings toward nurturing and enlarging the money relation. To hang the future of the totality on thisness is to overlook the center's true causal dependencies. It is also to foreclose the center's boundless curative potential. Instead of setting aesthetic redemption against monetary alienation as critical theory has done in the past, I call upon the aesthetic's much disputed saving powers to assist in actualizing money's social potential. In this project, I remain committed to aesthetic expansion and its social potential, but such expansions must sit squarely within the world that money mediates. They must *realize* rather than *resist* the money relation. The aesthetic must seek to enlarge, not escape, money's own expansive field.

Finally, I should clarify: my claim is that not simply that MMT opens the history of modern money and aesthetics to untapped utopian possibilities for public spending and social care. Rather, my contention is an emphatically normative one. MMT shows that money's status as a centralized and unrestricted government utility never ceases to structure social production, that it does so as a matter of everyday operational reality. Whether or not this occurs consciously or well remains an urgent question. But no amount of disavowal or negligence can erase the empirical effects of money's boundless public center on modern history. As a result, MMT forces us to think of money's utopian and normative dimensions as inextricably intertwined.

The Royal Road to the Neoliberal Unconscious

This leads us back to where we began: the conspicuous convergence of money, physics, and aesthetics in contemporary action media. I opened with a brief analysis of *Spectre* not merely because the film crystallizes the toxic contradictions that organize neoliberal money relations. I do so because *Spectre* exemplifies the action aesthetics that define the neoliberal order and because the sublime haecceity that quavers at the center of such media plays a pivotal role in my argument about the history of modern money and aesthetics.

My first claim is that these media physics provide a royal road to the neoliberal unconscious. Arising along with the turn to neoliberal economic governance during the late 1970s, such media physics take initial shape in the immersive "thrill ride" aesthetics of the New Hollywood blockbuster pioneered by Steven Spielberg, George Lucas, and Lucas's special effects house Industrial Light and Magic.[7] Pre-1970s Hollywood admitted, emphasized, and exploited the moving-picture medium's uncanny abstractness. So-called Classical Hollywood assumed a homogeneous visual grammar during this period and produced a relatively stable and seamless space-time that film scholars have labeled the "continuity system."[8] Nonetheless, Classical Hollywood was hailed as the "dream factory" and cinematic experience regarded as hallucinatory and ephemeral. Especially when it came to special effects, or "trick shots," pre-1970s Hollywood variously delighted in screen action's spatial indeterminacy and temporal evanescence.

In contrast to earlier Hollywood action aesthetics, post-1970s Hollywood labors to ground screen action physically in a material here-and-now. It does so, moreover, by anchoring the sensorium in a deeply immersive phenomenology that film scholar Frederick Wasser has dubbed a "you are there" feeling.[9] An intensive thisness thus organizes films from *Close Encounters of the Third Kind* (1977) to *Gravity* (2015). It also informs a parallel yet distinct history of mainstream video games. Films fracture the old continuity system and shift the locus of continuity from an insecure visual field to bass-driven sensations of locomotion. Games, too, rely upon sound to bring mass and weight to digital appearances, though their sustained and often jarring perspectives tend to break from classical continuity in ways new media theorist Alexander Galloway links to cinematic tropes of irrationality and psychosis.[10] In any case, nearly all action media suppress screen movement's fundamentally abstract character. At the same time, they fetishize hi-tech abstraction in their production processes and diegetic worlds. What is more, by contracting experience around sensations of friction, falling, and impact, such media comport the senses toward a sublime material flux that variously fills up and withdraws from the perceptual field like some capricious god.

Post-1970s action physics become *the* dominant aesthetic mode in an age known for diversifying practices, niches, and preferences. Treated largely uncritically by film media and scholars and eschewed by serious aesthetes, these action physics nevertheless become a ritualized site of convergence and repair for a fractured social body. On my analysis, such media both amplify and reify the phenomenology that rules neoliberal money relations. Orienting the sensorium toward a sublime haecceity—a materially expansive nearness, or *propinquity*—action media teach spectators and players to subordinate abstraction to physics and seek salvation in an erratic material flux. For this reason, action media at once hyperbolize and naturalize neoliberalism's abstract money physics, eliminating both the sense of abstraction's curative capacities and an awareness of the boundless public center that coordinates collective life.

By the same token, these media physics are also profoundly meaningful. Far from vacant ideology or brute domination, these forms compose rich and varied expressions along the lines of what film and media scholar Amy Rust has called "figures."[11] Figures are never empty or just brutal, Rust shows in her study of late 1960s and early 1970s cinematic violence. Rather, figures are deeply historical emanations that teem with both sensation *and* social sense. In the case of post-1970s action physics, figural returns to material propinquity represent a symptom of collective crisis. As symptoms, psychoanalysis reminds us, such repetitions work to thwart social transformation. But as both Rust and psychoanalysis equally discern, symptoms contribute to the very texture of the real and express genuine historical suffering. Such is the nature of the symptomatic haecceity that drives neoliberal action media. Its figurations lend variable shape to the neoliberal order, even as they prevent things from appearing otherwise. More important, they harbor cryptic yearnings for deliverance that demand this otherwise be heard and answered. My book is written in response to these yearnings. Its project is less to critique the reifying logics of action media than to uncover collective attachments to neoliberalism's "you are there" and reverse the social deprivation its figures hold in place.

My second claim about post-1970s screen action follows from the first. With their simulated implosion of formal abstraction and material propinquity, neoliberal action physics play a vital role in reifying not only the neoliberal monetary imagination but also the traditional money/aesthetics narrative. Under neoliberalism, a generalized collapse of abstraction and propinquity unfolds in the nominally separate realms of money and aesthetics. In the domain of political economy, the mid-1970s represents the moment when the Bretton Woods gold standard established at the close of the Second World War is dismantled and money is once and for all untethered from any metaphysical attachments to precious metals. The fatal twist of this shift is that money is affirmed as an abstract technology backed solely by political decree, or so-called fiat, at the same time that it is also envisioned as an alienable thisness that perpetually exceeds government capture and control. Under former metal standards, a perceived gap between monetary abstraction and its material substrate permitted the money relation to be contested occasionally. During the nineteenth century, for instance, critical intellectuals and political movements pointed to differences between what money was and the producibility of gold, silver, and paper dollars. As such, they politicized the gap between what money is and what it can be.[12] The neoliberal period eradicates this distinction; it presumes money's abstract status. Rather than reveal money's public center, however, neoliberal political economy paradoxically treats monetary abstraction like a contracted and alienable thing. In consequence, money is banished to a realm of material propinquity, making it impossible to contest its construction.

In the domain of aesthetics, the neoliberal period finds critical theorists declaring more or less defunct the once-utopian strivings of aesthetic modernism and avant-gardism, which had given formal and technical abstractions pride of place. "Abstract art . . . creates new types of spatial relationships, new inventions of forms, new visuals laws," propounded artist and Bauhaus school member László Moholy-Nagy. "[It is] the visual counterpart to a more purposeful, cooperative human society."[13] Inverting such formulas, Theodor Adorno transformed abstraction into a type of negative illumination that turns the indeterminacy of monetary abstraction toward the aesthetic's more reparative ends. "If in monopoly capitalism it is primarily exchange value . . . that is consumed," writes Adorno, "in the modern artwork it is its abstractness, that irritating indeterminateness of what it is and to what purpose it is, that becomes a cipher of what the work is."[14] Conversely, aestheticians in the neoliberal era imagine abstraction's alterity increasingly absorbed by monetary abstraction. Nearly every aspect of collective experience is subsumed, according to Fredric Jameson, by the "bewildering new world space of late or multinational capital."[15] This total subsumption of collective existence is supposed to make the historical antagonism between money and aesthetics all but obsolete. Like a slow-motion film depicting the shutdown of Rust Belt machinery, the dialectical machinery of modernity's money/aesthetics opposition grinds to an interminable finish. With genuine exteriority to monetary abstraction made untenable, contemporary aesthetic interventions are forced to situate themselves within and against what critics regularly envision as capital's "global flows." As a result, both the neoliberalization of money and the neoliberalization of the aesthetic converge in an abstract money physics. The neoliberal age forfeits abstraction's formal and technical potential for the private sphere and flees to relations of material propinquity to confront the privation now associated with all types of abstraction.

Between these parallel developments in political economy and aesthetics, post-1970s action physics are surprisingly central. Still, to understand their role, it is essential to consider the shifting social significance of formal and technical abstraction in the late twentieth century. The neoliberal period saw midcentury modernism's utopian and often technocratic faith in abstraction give way to postmodern or so-called contemporary aesthetics, wherein abstraction became increasingly associated with the private sphere and neoliberal pleasures and privations. Coming after the disappointments of an earlier utopian European modernism, the midcentury abstractions of International Style Architecture, Abstract Expressionism, and Space Age kitsch emblematized the era's state-supported project of white middle-class uplift. However limited, contradictory, or repressive this project seems in retrospect, midcentury modernism's embrace of formal and technical abstraction nonetheless conveyed, I argue, a complex investment in monetary abstraction and its capacities to order and elevate collective life.

During late 1960s and early 1970s the limits and failures of the midcentury's sexist and racist military industrial complex became increasingly apparent to both Left and Right. Amid political pressures from the New Left and the Nixonian backlash, aesthetic and cultural producers presented myriad challenges to midcentury modernism's particular faith in abstraction. Mainstream cultural production organized matter and meaning in disruptive new ways, be it experimental multitrack pop music, post-Code Hollywood filmmaking, or Fluxus and post-minimalist art. A contradictory ethos soon emerged, however, that would redefine 1970s political economy and the neoliberal relationship to formal and technical abstraction that followed. On one hand, the New Deal era's state-cultivated abundance was replaced by a widely hailed "age of limits." Whether explicitly or implicitly, this rhetoric falsely linked allegedly profligate fiscal expenditures to problems of inflation, overconsumption, state violence, and environmental degradation. On the other hand, the 1970s announced a new era of cultural diversity and individual expression. The result was that while the 1970s constricted the capacities of monetary abstraction through fiscal austerity, high interest rates, and anti-labor policies, the pleasures of the aesthetic and especially of emphatically abstract aesthetics were reborn under the banner of neoliberal privatization. Whereas the abstractions of midcentury modernism became associated with technocratic domination and homogeneity, emergent forms of expression and abstraction became signifiers of a social order organized around public impoverishment and private transformation. Different forms of expression might strive to promote or resist the prevailing order. Yet no form would be produced outside its constricted monetary relation or contest money's metaphysical reduction to an abstract physics. All forms would bear the signature of neoliberal privation.

This contradiction comes to a head in the dominant culture's changing relationship to formal and technical abstraction. From personalized electronics to a speculative art market, a neoliberal age ruled by Wall Street and Silicon Valley tied the abstractions of data, design, and display to precarious private thrills. This means that the genuinely expansive and transformative powers of abstraction to transcend relations of material propinquity become wedded to a permanent state of uncertainty and suffering. In an unconscious, yet nonetheless direct response to these difficulties, Wall Street and Silicon Valley inspired and often directly funded the physics-obsessed action films and games that now permeate neoliberal culture. Thus, while abstraction's imaginative and curative capacities were relinquished to private capital, private capital itself came to devote tremendous energies to creating a popular aesthetics grounded in a reassuring material propinquity.

The upshot is a symptomatic loop that reverses the order of its construction and makes alternative political economies unimaginable. When one begins from the physicalist phenomenology that post-1970s action media engenders, material propinquity seems prior to abstraction, and finite matter appears the literal ground of meaning. This feeling of material finitude then fuels a deep-seated ambivalence toward the technical and formal abstractions that the private sphere apparently and unproblematically celebrates. Finally, by treating material finitude as a ground for meaning and by stoking ambivalence toward all types of abstraction, post-1970s action physics engender comportments to the world that make the structure of monetary abstraction indiscernible.

For this reason, I argue that post-1970s action physics synthesize the converging tendencies we see in post–Bretton Woods fiat money and critical aesthetics. These action media do not represent or merely embody the transition to neoliberalism. Rather, they perform a crucial historical labor in their own right. They quite literally *substantiate* this era's imagined implosions of abstraction and material propinquity in the form of a popularly enjoyed Gestalt. They complete the supposed convergence of money and aesthetics thought to define the neoliberal period and reify the dialectical narrative that frames it. As a result, post-1970s action media should be regarded as the unrecognized social epicenter of the neoliberal turn. Indeed, more than the era's explicit accounts of money, and far more than any abstruse aesthetic theory, neoliberal action physics train the senses at a precognitive and prediscursive level. In so doing, they usher forth a worldview that relegates abstraction's social potential to private commerce. They accept material propinquity as the unquestioned ground from which to confront neoliberal insecurity. And they make unimaginable any alternative relationship between political economy and sensory life. As such, it may be said that post-1970s action physics stiffen a knot tied long ago by the hegemonic money/aesthetics dialectic. Without recourse to concepts or words, such media physics transform a tangled modern promise into a tightening neoliberal noose.

My third and final claim about neoliberal action media cuts to my core contention in *Declarations of Dependence*: post-1970s action media open a previously unseen historical passageway, or wormhole, that links neoliberalism's dead-end dialectic between money and aesthetics to the enshrouded origins of this dialectic in early modernity. I trace these origins to the historical rise of modern haecceity in Italy's late medieval city-states and to the Liberal political economy these metaphysics came to authorize. Approached from MMT's heterodox conception of money, or what I am calling money's boundless public center, these origins reveal themselves afresh. Situating the traditional money/aesthetics dialectic in the context of an emergent thisness and an incipient Liberal political economy, *Declarations of Dependence* reconstructs the historical relationship between money and aesthetics. Uncovering a more salutatory metaphysics, it severs the noose of neoliberalism and envisions new supports for the collectivity I wish to release.

Modernity's Unreconciled Origins

The source of the historical dialectic that terminates with neoliberal action media, I have suggested, lies in the social and political turmoil of northern Italy during the thirteenth, fourteenth, and fifteenth centuries. Specifically, the essential features of the modern relationship between money and the aesthetic can be traced to the remarkable economic and cultural life of the late medieval city-state. At first blush, today's internationally connected and hi-tech political economy seems to share little with the comparatively localized and pre-industrial world of Renaissance Florence. Moreover, what British Sentimentalists and German Idealists would later imagine as a quasi-autonomous aesthetic sphere was largely absent in the Florentine context. If anything, the primary tension in the period stretching from 1350 to 1500 was between money and morality, commerce and spirituality, economic life and the life of the church.

Still, money and what we call the aesthetic remained bed-fellows during this period. Humanist apologists for Florentine elites boasted about the role of the rich in provisioning artworks for both civic and church institutions. This, along with com-plaints of papal profligacy, led to conflicts between money's purportedly corrupting influence and the church as institutional center of morality. A contradictory wellspring for contemporary relationships to money and aesthetics, early modern Florence also supplied the budding metaphysics of *haecceitas* that first shaped a proto-Liberal political economy and an ontology of money as alienable thisness. Prior to this transformation, an explicitly nonproximate, or transcendent, causality held sway over the late medieval intellectual order. Developed furthest by scholastic theologians such as Albertus Magnus and Thomas Aquinas, this causality begins with a boundless center occu-pied by God and the Universal Church. It then conceptualizes change through the relation of nonproximate copresences, which realize the center's potential through finite local activities that never exhaust God's endless abundance. From the twelfth to fourteenth centuries, this transcendent causality informed the operation and theorization of the papal money system under which the northern Italian city-states grew. In northern Europe, where the principles arising from the Thomist tradition received some of their most compelling practical applications, jurists such as Henry de Bracton argued that sovereign governance constituted the center of economic relations. They also insisted on what they deemed the "sacredness" of the public purse, or "fisc," which was infinite, ubiquitous, and inalienable.[16]

Beginning in the fourteenth century, however, challenges to this vision began to emerge. Thomism's transcendent causality was spurned for an immanent *haecceitas*, first by Franciscan nominalists such as Duns Scotus and William of Ockham and, later, by humanists of the Florentine tradition like Petrarch and Lorenzo Valla. This immanent *haecceitas* informed Florence's libertine ethos of free associationism, which imagined discrete interactions between embodied agents as the sole source of causality, meaning, and value.[17] It also drove Florence into a war against the pope during which the city-state fought for both political and economic sovereignty.[18] The Florentine Republic triumphed against the papacy but at an enormous cost. Instead of assuming their freshly won right to a boundless sovereign purse, the wealthy guilds that dominated the Florentine system propped the newly independent Republic on haecceity's immanent associations and, worse, on an order that made money a private and finite thing that moved in and out of physical locales. Limiting fiscal spending to tax revenues and bond sales, the republic predicated its social order on an alienable thisness instead of a boundless public account. This hallucinatory alienability brought with it a hallucinatory threat of loss, haunting Florentine society with spectacles of disintegration that threatened to deplete public coffers and dismantle public life.

Responding to money's spectacles of disintegration, art and religious culture offered anxious sites of material reparation and religious salvation. Florence became the center of Renaissance art and humanist philosophy as well as a historically novel ethos of artistic freedom and individual genius. Characterized by substantialized experiences of a replete here-and-now, this culture contracted sensory faculties around a full and comparatively secure materiality. This materiality promised to open the sensorium to forces beyond the here-and-now. Yet it also furnished the subject with a protective envelope that stabilized a haecceity that otherwise appeared to be giving way. Cutting across the artistic and cultural practices of the Florentine Renaissance, this operation became especially concentrated in visual artifacts such as fresco, tempera, and later, oil painting. Geometrical perspective, in particular, moved Florentine art away from the transcendent causality of Byzantine and Gothic arrangements and toward a hazardous grounding in sensations of material gravity. This gravitropic visuality, as I call it, answered spectacles of disintegration with gravity's assuring embrace.

Thus, while my argument is hardly novel in presenting Renaissance Florence and Quattrocento perspective as central to modernity, my attention to their haecceity shifts the historical significance of perspectivalism from visual verisimilitude to gravitropic phenomenology. Long recognized for its pursuit of mimetic likeness, or the so-called *imitatio naturae* principle, Quattrocento perspective supposedly derived from the structure of nature. With parallel lines that converged at one or more vanishing points, it promised to open a transparent window onto the embodied relations of the real world. Suspicious of the viewpoint perspectivalism produces, Marxist aestheticians have historically underscored its links to the possessive individualism of modern life. Such arguments follow Marxist critiques of money in that they accuse an abstract form of naturalizing social domination and economic alienation. The abstractions of Renaissance perspective carve out a disembodied and idealized position of mastery for the viewing subject to whom they extend an illusion of transparency. The result allows the bourgeois subject to imagine holding dominion over the world and possessing myriad objects. As in Marxist critiques of money, however, the dubious mathematics of Renaissance perspective in fact dominate the subject they establish and alienate its illusory viewpoint from connections to the material and social world.

On my reading, Renaissance perspective is neither "natural" nor "abstract," and the historical significance of Quattrocento pictorialism has little to do with oppositions between transparency and opacity. Instead, I argue, Renaissance perspective constructs a gravitropic phenomenology that aims to ground viewer and viewed securely in a relationship of material propinquity—no matter how stable or unstable, transparent or opaque, that relation may appear. This phenomenology places the spectatorial body in the material here-and-now of a geometrically projected scene. More important, it physically anchors the embodied viewpoint in a distributed array of light and heavy figures suggesting a world held together by forces of gravitational attraction that include the viewing position itself. This overlooked phenomenology harbors a gravitropic wish—a wish to realize what money rooted in haecceity desires but cannot accomplish: *to secure social mediation at a distance.* In the face of money's alienable thisness, gravitropic visuality cradles the viewer in its all-encompassing material grasp. It mediates social relations between near and far, seen and unseen, and does so while abjuring what Valla dismissed as the "weightless ravings" of scholastic terminology.[19] With this, Renaissance perspective's gravitropic phenomenology redeems the anemic haecceity that organizes the money relation in the Florentine Republic. By rendering haecceity a totalizing and all-inclusive relation of material propinquity, Quattrocento perspective at once reduces relationality to contiguity and imagines that this contiguity is capable of holding the social order together.

In the centuries that followed, Renaissance-era conflicts between money and morality slowly transmuted into a recognizably modern dialectic between money and aesthetics. Still, it is the gravitropic wish made palpable by Florence's enduring visual culture that contained the secret to this dialectic's still-unreconciled origins. The modern process begins when, in the midst of religious strife and war, elites in the Dutch republic and England suppressed lingering philosophical and legal arguments for money's sovereign inalienability. They adopted a Florentine-like money form based on haecceity and deployed it at a far grander scale. The Dutch and English *internationalized* haecceity, in other words, first through the former's break with the Spanish Empire in the late sixteenth century and, later, the latter's founding of the Bank of England in 1694. In each case, a growing bourgeoisie established a new type of economic order, one that treated money as a private and alienable thisness that restricted government spending to finite tax revenues and bond sales. As a consequence, production increased and social life transformed. Rather than mobilize a boundless public fisc to employ and care for everyone, however, it gave rise to ongoing financial instability, mass unemployment, poverty, and starvation. Indeed, in spite of its gains, the money form's haecceity brought metaphysical uncertainty to modern thought and life.

In the Dutch context René Descartes inaugurated modern philosophy with haecceity as an unquestioned yet decidedly anxious metaphysical ground. In *Mediations on First Philosophy* (1641), the French émigré staged a now legendary encounter with a melting piece of wax, which served to demonstrate the untrustworthiness of the material world. Answering this unreliability, Descartes appealed to the purported certainty of abstract mathematics and rational cognition.[20] In the process, however, his melting wax stamped haecceity's spectacle of disintegration on the soul of modernity's rational subject. Hardly born with Descartes, his metaphysical drama was well known to Dutch speculators during the "Tulip Mania" market bubble of 1637 as well as to the thousands faced with unreasonable bread prices as a result. More broadly, it was familiar to Calvinist multitudes whose identities were shaped by what, from a contemporary perspective, was a series of tax revolts against extractive papal tithes and indulgences. Still, it is Descartes who makes a hemorrhaging haecceity the foundation for a "first philosophy" and for heralding a new age of metaphysics forged in contingency, uncertainty, and volatility. Descartes paved the way for a modern regime of knowing that refused transcendent causalities and struggled to find its bearings in the erratic thisness of an immanent here-and-now.

John Locke, for example, roots the operations of reason in contiguous associations among individual ideas.[21] Locke's epistemology strives at once to know and stabilize worldly relations via the thisness of specific ideas and the haecceity of the associations generated when individual ideas meet. Unsurprisingly, these same metaphysics also inform Locke's philosophy of money, which attempts to balance modern economic relations on the thisness of individual agents and the heredity of their allegedly free associations. Writers such as Adam Smith develop this balancing act yet further. Building on the ideas of Descartes, Locke, and Isaac Newton, Smith refashioned the imagination into a faculty for envisaging hidden links between disjointed appearances. In so doing, he not only attributed haecceity to individuals and associations but also installed it in the intervals he imagined to exist between material beings and relations.[22] In Smith's account the positive substance or force that fills these intervals matters less than his presumption that some contiguous element holds the universe in place. It is the task of the imagination to confront these gaps and speculate about the underlying material relations that govern the universe. As a site of metaphysical ordering, this invisible contiguous interval permits Smith to imagine money as a relatively autonomous field made of myriad imperceptible exchanges.[23] Smith's "invisible hand" fills out the gaps in the field of exchange and brings with it a sense of order and balance. Thus, while he sees the market as an imperfect system that requires government's visible support, Smith nonetheless reduces the whole of political economy to a problem of haecceity. He does not engage its boundlessness as a public center that organizes and supports inalienable, non-contiguous relations.

Skeptical philosophy maintains Smith's commitment to thisness as a paradoxical remedy to the precariousness of haecceity. David Hume affirms, for instance, the power of reason despite its dependency on a fleeting and untrustworthy here-and-now. Evacuating metaphysical categories such as substance, force, and selfhood, Hume relies on irony to subvert any widely accepted claims to metaphysical certainty.[24] In this sense the Scotsman realizes the destruction of metaphysical principles initiated by his predecessor Scotus. Like his precursors, moreover, Hume demonstrates a tenacious commitment to the metaphysics of haecceity, one that escapes his corrosive irony. His devotion to thisness likewise orients Hume's influential contributions to modern political economy. Most notably, haecceity grounds Hume's well-known "species-flow" theory of international trade. According to this theory, laissez-faire governance is supposed to ensure an even distribution of money and goods between states on the analogy of a fluid passing back and forth between contiguous chambers.[25] With this, Hume makes a finite physical flow between nation-states the central mechanism responsible for production and distribution.

It is Marx, however, who goes furthest in grounding critique in haecceity. Rather than attuning critique to the ways that monetary governance actively organizes precariousness and poverty across disparate spaces, or railing against the state for creating mass unemployment and financial instability, Marx derides earlier juridical arguments for money's fiat status, calling them "sycophantic service [to] crowned heads."[26] He develops an elaborate poetics of capital that, by turns, vilifies and eroticizes money's estranging movements. Money is a "fetish," according to Marx.[27] It combines religious obfuscation and primitivist charms and transmutes a material relationship between persons into an alienating movement of things. Money is also a "crystal of value."[28] This crystal is supposed to siphon "surplus value" from the populace as it traverses geographic spaces. "Vampire-like, capital only lives by sucking living labor," writes Marx, one of many appeals to Gothic monsters.[29] Money is a "chemical bond" that destroys living bonds and does so through "monstrous exactions."[30] It creates "abysses," "earthquakes," and "volcanic eruptions."[31] Money, in Marx's hands, is haecceity at its most unmanageable and unmoored.

Of course, the objective of Marxist poetics is never to conflate sign and referent, word and thing. It is to make money's imperceptible haecceity feel viscerally present so as to denounce Smith's benign interval for its essential privation and injustice. This is, in fact, how we ought to read the metaphorical thrust of *The Communist Manifesto* (1848): "All fixed, fast-frozen relations . . . are swept away," and "all that is solid melts into air."[32] If such slogans now read as archetypical of modern experience, it is neither because they literally depict money's operations nor because they describe money's concrete effects. It is because *as figures*, Marx's spectacles of disintegration go furthest to express the calamitous haecceity around which the modern era has come to revolve.

Accordingly, when British Sentimentalists and German Idealists first set sensibility, culture, and art against the money relation, they tendered the aesthetic as a concerted response to the concrete alienations and volatilities that Marx describes and money appears to condition. Yet in truth, I argue, the aesthetic first arose as an answer to the Liberal metaphysics of money and its disintegrating haecceity and only secondarily as a response to money's concrete historical effects. As Liberal money's harrowing thisness threatened persons with privation, constricted action, and social isolation, the aesthetic formed a counterimage of collective belonging that was heterogeneous, replete, and strove for universal communion. In this taken-for-granted striving, however, the aesthetic project meets its historical limit. That limit, I contend, is the modern metaphysics of haecceity, the gravitropic visuality of which—from Florentine perspective to neoliberal action media—holds the key for assessing how to overcome the limits of monetary and aesthetic thisness.

The Basis of Social Security

More than any form of artistic experience, gravitropic visuality reveals the essence and limit of the modern aesthetic project. Expressing a wish for haecceity to live up to its promise, the gravitropic aesthetic articulates collective desires for a social bond that is not only materially contiguous but also proves capable of securing far-flung persons and things in its all-encompassing grip. The aesthetic is, precisely, the promise of haecceity *writ large*. Modernity's overinvestment in thisness, meanwhile, is where gravitropism finds its limit. The aesthetic is limited because its overinvestment in haecceity arises at the expense of the transcendent tethers that wed a governing body to currency users. The money relation is, after all, a social obligation that orchestrates activity at a distance, not a contiguous physics that pushes this way and the other. Indeed, no amount of sensuous abundance or fellow feeling in the here-and-now can transform that obligation's essential structure or reorganize the boundless public center that conditions it. Money always outstrips the aesthetic in terms of scope, capacity, and social responsibility.

In a way, we can say the aesthetic marks a threshold beyond which haecceity prevents any concerted social activity from expanding. It designates the full extension of haecceity's saving powers. The aesthetic is nothing but that frontier's very name.

The imperative of critical theory in the wake of MMT, then, is to lay bare the deprived haecceity that frames modernity's contradictory dialectic of money and aesthetics. It must also labor to redeem this relationship by opening both money and the aesthetic to the center's limitless curative potential. In the end, the aesthetic's investments in sensuous communion still matter for collective life. Before its promise can be realized, however, we must first grapple with the fact that the aesthetic project arose as an embodiment of, rather than a genuine antidote to, the privation of Liberal money's disintegrating thisness. I take modernity's gravitropic visuality as the site for this intervention. I transform its constrictive physics into a site for transcendence by disclosing its immanent connection to the boundless public center it forecloses.

To do so, it is necessary not only to place MMT's ontology of money at the heart of critical theory but also to rearticulate critique's essential question and methodological concern. What I propose, therefore, is a shift in critique from problems of *power* to questions of *care*. From the Frankfurt School to the diverse fields of inquiry that emerge during and after poststructuralism, critical theory generally takes Liberal money's privation for granted. With this assumption, it focuses primarily on the social domination authorized by money's abstract value. Then, in a variety of complex and often implicit ways, critical theory posits its own practice as an alternative method for looking after the totality. In this sense, critical theory foregrounds complexities of power and treats conundrums of caretaking as secondary. When critical theory does engage care's difficulties, moreover, it generally emphasizes localized associations that resist the present order. In this sense it seeks to release caretaking from monetary obligations. My project, by contrast, radically restructures the way money organizes care from within the social totality.

There is, of course, an important exception to the foregoing depreciation of care in the Marxo-feminist "wages against housework" movement that flourished in Italy and the United States during 1970s and after. Though its proponents left the privation of the Liberal money form unquestioned, Selma James, Silvia Federici, and others nonetheless joined radical critique with demands for compensating and reorganizing unpaid care work. Also notable in this regard are the contributions of mid-twentieth-century African American intellectuals and organizers. From Bayard Rustin and Dr. Martin Luther King Jr. to Coretta Scott King and the Black Panther Party, this tradition carried out incisive critiques of political economy while making radical calls for government-supported full employment, socialized day care, public housing, and the like. These movements proceeded from the problem of care and made demands for change that seem incompatible with the Liberal view of money. From the perspective of MMT, however, they appear imminently realizable.

Yet for the most part, the Liberal money form's presumed privation has led critical theorists to forfeit questions of care for the whole in the here-and-now. Such questions find little place in rigorous theoretical engagements with the social order that money mediates. Instead, critical theory treats the exigencies of care from the perspective of resistance movements that strive to escape the money relation altogether. In projecting critique beyond the extant operations of public accounting, however, critical theory blinds itself to money's limitless curative potential and relinquishes care's riddles to Liberal reformers. Contracting the sphere of care to Liberal modernity's limited haecceity, it renders care an activity that must oppose present power relations rather than proceed from within them. As a consequence, critical theory tends to exculpate itself from answering the difficulties of collective caretaking in the present. It pursues a liberated and expansive haecceity that Marx deemed a "direct" organization of "freely associated labor" and Max Horkheimer later described as an "association of free men in which each has the possibility of self-development."[33] But the problem with this model of care is that it derives from the aesthetic's own impoverished haecceity. As in the traditional conception of the aesthetic, this narrow model of care concentrates on cultivating the sensuous thisness of immediate filiations, either in the midst of current struggles or by holding out an image of a future in which all relations appear as such. It thereby externalizes the difficulties that constitute the present totality and exculpates critical praxis from answering the burden of care in its widest breadth.

Critique after MMT sidesteps the prevailing tendency to set domination against a liberated and seemingly more caring haecceity beyond the money relation. As I deploy it, MMT grounds critique in the exigencies of the present monetary obligation, which establishes interdependent and distinctly noncontiguous relationships between currency-issuing governments and the persons and environs money organizes. More important, MMT permits me to install what I call the *mystery of care* at the center of the money relation and to insist that this mystery is irreducible to the problems of power that have historically oriented critical theory. By care, I mean something different from the dominant modern understanding of this term as an empathic being-for-others that one adopts or refuses. Rather, I recover care's original and richer meaning as an anxious and inescapable social obligation and a form of collective cultivation and uplift. On one hand, care is an unshirkable charge, which tethers every person to the social totality and does so in a manner that is prior to questions of individual consent or moral activity.

On the other hand, it constitutes an undetermined activity of cultivating the social totality. Always at issue and never self-evident, care composes that mysterious intersection where a radical sense of implication meets radical transformability and where the social order as a whole hangs in the balance.

In modernity, this mystery is to be found nowhere other than in money's boundless public center. Money is *the* locus of care's inescapable question: How are we to cultivate our world? In order to alter how the boundless center poses and answers this question, care must become critical theory's primary domain of concern. To subordinate care to power is to disavow the ways in which care never ceases to create and unsettle the world that power inhabits. It is to reduce the mystery of social reproduction to a tellurian force that waxes and wanes. Subordinating care to power passes over the ways in which even the most brutal power relations implicate everyone in the maintenance of a cruel world. Above all, it closes the money relation's contested infinitude. Critique after MMT must hold that infinitude open—not as an end itself but as a new and radically expanded foundation for politics and the fight for political power.

MMT has set forth a rational critique of the dominant political and economic order. Appealing to logical argumentation, it proffers a counter-rationality that seeks to uncover the irrationality of the reigning doxa. Still, this counter-rationality tends to bewilder and dismay the majority of persons it addressees. The confusion does not result from lack of clarity on the part of MMT writings. It does not involve semantic inconsistencies between different discursive regimes. Instead, it is a consequence of MMT's deep unseating of the metaphysics of haecceity that have made modern money intelligible. One sees attachments to haecceity in the discourse of heterodox economists who have shown sympathy to or even become associated with MMT. Marxist economist and former embattled Greek finance minister

Yanis Varoufakis, for example, has presented papers alongside MMT economists at myriad conferences and openly avowed MMT's insights into the nature of fiat money. In his well-known book *The Global Minotaur* (2011), however, as well as other writings, Varoufakis predicates his analyses on what he calls a "surplus recycling mechanism."[34] Conceived as a kind of hydraulic physics that takes liquid in and pushes it out, this surplus recycling mechanism is supposed to transport money from one region to another and thereby "redistribute" value to the world's economies. As any MMT economist will tell you, money is a debit/credit system, an instrument of simultaneously marking and accounting, not an alienable chit that can be redistributed. Thus, while Varoufakis wholly accepts that money is an unlimited public account, his unrelenting and seemingly unconscious attachment to haecceity prevents him from perceiving political economy according to the view MMT makes available.

As most public presentations by MMT economists demonstrate, this attachment to money's thisness is not only stubborn; it also stirs up anxiety. For instance, MMT economist Randall L. Wray delivered a talk in Spain in 2015 at the invitation of Asociación de Economía Crítica, the Madrid chapter of the Association for the Taxation of Financial Transactions and Aid to Citizens (ATTAC).[35] During the talk Wray explained that a monetarily sovereign state need neither tax nor borrow before it spends. Such a state can always afford any social program it wishes to implement. Wray warned, however, that Eurozone rules have robbed member states of their fiscal sovereignty. For this reason, Spain must exit the Euro currency's punishing fiscal restrictions before it can spend as needed on public employment, social security, and other urgent programs. After Wray's presentation, a thoughtful undergraduate student in the audience offered some reflections. "This has been incredibly enlightening," she pronounced, as she proceeded to rehearse some of the ideas Wray previously conveyed. Still, said the student, something was preventing her from comprehending the full significance of Wray's presentation. In an effort to clarify her puzzlement, she asked Wray the following, though her tone suggested she knew the question would not prove illuminating. "What else is there to finance . . . social security," she queried, "if we are *not* to rely on taxes?"

The Spanish student's perplexity is not exceptional. This type of anxious questioning regularly follows presentations of MMT's key claims. Still, the *form* of this particular student's question is telling for the way it announces the metaphysical unease MMT's intervention inspires. Specifically, it indicates the fundamental question that accompanies this heterodox school when it enters public discourse. "What else is there to finance . . . social security if we are *not* to rely on taxes?" One can restate the inquiry as follows: Without the unnamable thisness that taxes are supposed to embody, where can we locate the *source* of public spending? To put a finer point on it, the question might finally be stated: *When money is stripped of the haecceity on which it is imagined to hinge, on what basis is social security supposed to rely?*

The fact that this more fundamental question has neither been asked nor answered suggests that MMT's rational methodology is insufficient to the challenge at hand. It is insufficient precisely because it has thus far neglected to thematize, let alone explicitly critique, the metaphysics that have historically made modern money thinkable. The real challenge for critical theory, then, is not simply to assist MMT by replacing irrationalism with rationalism or by bringing economic clarity to neoliberal ignorance. Critical theory must conceive new ways of weaving the topology and tissue of the real. It must redefine what *counts* as real before that reality can be engaged as such. Only by intervening in this preconscious and unheard-of background is it possible to perceive money's boundless public center and put this center to work for one and all.

In this book I do not trace the linear account of the alternative history I have presented in my introduction. Rather, I pursue a series of critical interventions distributed across four chapters that unfold this history through a set of broader theoretical claims. Each intervention treats a key problem for critical theory while laboring to rethink the relationship between money and aesthetics from the early modern period to the neoliberal present. The four problems are: (1) the ontology of money; (2) the politics of care; (3) the metaphysics of mediation; and (4) the aesthetic's gravitropic phenomenology. In the end I argue that saving ourselves from social and ecological ruination requires risking money's enigmatic transubstantiations of matter and meaning rather than settling for the comforts of the aesthetic's gravitropic deliverance. In so doing, I show how the aesthetic remains vital to any critical praxis. Yet I insist that making good on the aesthetic's promise of redemption requires exposing the mystery of its sensuous expansions to money's incalculable grace.

1

Transcending the Aesthetic

*Can we forget the ideas of progress and dialectics by which,
in its own eyes, modern tradition has redeemed itself? If the
expression of modern tradition has a meaning—a paradoxical
meaning—the history of this modern tradition will be
contradictory and negative: it will be a story going nowhere.*
—Antoine Compagnon

*In the case of the King's tallies, Redemption Day was tax day
when the King's representative (the exchequer) arrived in the
village, spread cloth on the ground, and matched stock and
stub. Hallelujah, the tax was paid. The tally stick had value
because it could be used to "redeem" oneself on tax day.*
—L. Randall Wray

In the beginning of the modern era, there was money. The
aesthetic arose to mitigate money's insufficiencies. Various
modernisms and avant-gardes declared the split between political economy and aesthetics false and labored to sublate this
antagonism on the latter's terms.

Since then, however, historical avant-garde's defiant breach
of the levee protecting the aesthetic from everyday commerce
has been engulfed by an aestheticized money relation. Or so

the story goes. As Peter Bürger laments in his now canonical *Theory of the Avant-Garde* (1974), "During the time of the historical avant-garde movements, the attempt to do away with the distance between art and life still had all the pathos of historical progressiveness on its side. But in the meantime, the culture industry has brought about the false elimination of the distance between art and life, and this also allows one to recognize the contradictoriness of the avant-gardiste undertaking."[1] Some forty years later the same grand narrative seems to have accelerated and intensified for the worse. What Bürger's generation confronted as an uncontrollable flood now looks like a manageable tributary compared to the global deluge of today's hyperaestheticizing information capital.

Media theorist McKenzie Wark's account of hyperaestheticized commerce epitomizes the post-apocalyptic mood that colors the contemporary experience of this story. Wark is critical of information capital's seemingly total cooptation of the aesthetic. However, he abjures Bürger's nostalgia for modernity's lost dialectical gambit. Instead he confronts neoliberal capital's sensuous imagination straightaway, moving variously with and against its dizzying heterogeneity and boundary-crossing fluctuations.

> Today sophisticated techniques are gathering to make ever more complex projects instantly and constantly comparable and assessable—from refinancing News Corp. to invading a country to selling sneakers. The development of vectoral flows of information is what makes possible the space of flows, in which jobs, troops, money—anything—can be redirected from one interchangeable address to another. The aesthetic is part of this emergent terrain . . . whether it likes it or not. The vector enables an ever more rarefied *aesthetic economy.*[2]

Few contemporary aestheticians will adopt Wark's theoretical apparatus, which sees neoliberalism's digital and networked exchanges engendering a globalized space of potentially hackable "vectoral flows." Wark is not likely to face disagreement, however, in his grim diagnosis of information capitalism's "rarefied aesthetic economy."

That the aesthetic has become a primary vehicle for an unjust and uncontrollable global exchange regime is now a foregone conclusion. Somewhat paradoxically, this presumption underwrites a contemporary efflorescence in critical aesthetics, which continues to answer and reciprocally shape the neoliberal order it generally opposes. Despite an avowed opposition to neoliberal logics, contemporary aestheticians take as given the fact that the aesthetic no longer legitimately stands opposed to commerce. This is perhaps most marked in the work of critics who persist in making the case for aesthetic autonomy. For instance, Nicholas Brown maintains that "aesthetic autonomy today is . . . locked in a life or death struggle with the market."[3] Yet Brown distinguishes his assertion of autonomy *within* neoliberal aestheticization from the "rear-guard" sentimentalism that lingers in Bürger. Brown insists that the heroic enmity modernity posited between monetary and aesthetic spheres was itself more or less fallacious and that, fallacious or not, this historical antagonism is now buried in the past.

Despite such ritualized burials, the modern dialectic between money and aesthetics finds no resolution in the neoliberal period. Instead, modernity's failed dialectic sinks to the bottom of contemporary aesthetic consciousness, and its enduring irresolvability continues to orient critical encounters with neoliberalism's hyperaestheticized "flows." The crux of the problem is that while the social need to overcome monetary alienation intensifies in the neoliberal period, critical theory has developed no alternative to the money/aesthetics dialectic, and its past incapacity imbues present aesthetic thought with a dire relationship to the future. The result tends to undercut the contemporary aesthetic project with feelings of political hopelessness and historical fatigue. Thus, while the old dialectic between money and aesthetics may have lost its heroic promise, money's neoliberal triumph threatens theoretical interventions with social inconsequence and meaningful artistic practices with what critic Sven Lütticken has called "collector-pleasing irrelevance."[4]

In the present book I mean to redress this neoliberal malaise by rethinking the historical relationship between money and aesthetics from which it ascends. My primary contention is that the contemporary heterodox school of political economy called Modern Monetary Theory provides the critical leverage necessary for doing so. Whereas the hegemonic view treats money as a private, finite, and alienable *thisness*, MMT conceives money as a public, boundless, and politically answerable relationship that has the capacity to support every person and environment it mediates. The approach of MMT to political economy makes imaginable a host of transformative political projects. In this work I ask what MMT can do for critical theory and mobilize its intervention to answer the neoliberal era's political and aesthetic discontents.

Specifically, I contend that critical theory must transcend the utopian wager of the aesthetic's expansive and sensuous thisness if it is to advance beyond the historical deadlocks of the neoliberal era. It must embrace money's abstract boundless center as the source of social and ecological redemption. Modern aesthetics arose as a means to repair and resist the privations of the "Liberal money form," my term for the orthodox monetary ideology that dominates bourgeois modernity. Rather than treat the root of monetary alienation, the resulting antinomy between the economic and the aesthetic foreclosed money's emphatically abstract capacity to cultivate a sensuous, diverse, and open communality. In this book I labor to overcome the aesthetic's dialectical foreclosure of money's cultivating powers and set both political economy and what remains of the aesthetic project on money's more salubrious grounds.

In what follows I first present a critique of the Liberal money form and explicate the seemingly intractable difficulties it introduces into modern life. Next I outline the aesthetic project's answer to Liberal money's historical deficiencies and mark the political hopelessness that overtakes this project in the neoliberal era. Finally I devote the remainder of the chapter to explicating MMT's alternative account of the money relation, laying the groundwork for reconceiving the modern dialectic between money and aesthetics.

The Original Cell of Exchange

To grasp MMT's break with the prevailing orthodoxy, it is necessary to reconsider critically the traditional story of money that both Left and Right have historically presupposed. In the conventional account, money is taken to be a medium of exchange. Originating in primitive barter relations and maturing into place-bound markets, money in the traditional narrative is a token of exchange facilitating free trade between private individuals. This token functions as a representation of exchanged goods. It also operates as a contract that works according to the logic of the promise. I pledge you my money; you promise me a gallon of milk, an oil change, or monthly Internet service. Still, this mutual pledge is a risky affair, since it hinges solely on the mutual faith of the contracting parties. It is the token's specifically mathematical or abstract form, meanwhile, that allows for such exchange in the first place. Only by subsuming heterogeneous matters under the sign of universal equivalence is money capable of drawing the world together and lubricating the commerce of all things. Such commerce, according to orthodoxy, unfolds outside sovereign governance. Multiple social actors and organizations attempt to claim sovereignty over the exchange relation or subordinate it to centralizing logics or monopolistic controls. Money remains a fundamentally decentered medium of exchange that belongs to embodied market interactions.[5]

These interactions become, moreover, the basis for divisions of labor, complex systems of production and profit, and the multiplication of wants. Labor enters exchange circuits, and with this, money becomes an extension of embodied effort and a store of value. I trade my money token for your commodity in the aforementioned example. Now I must earn this token by storing labor time through work for a private employer or by skimming surplus value from the labor of others. Profits rise and fall, capital circulates, and desires proliferate. Money migrates beyond local markets and moves about the globe. Finally, finance leaps into the fray and money's ambulatory exchanges are further unmoored from their terrestrial bases. Things begin harmlessly enough: finance enables more production by speculating on the success or failure of future production and exchange. But speculation begets more speculation in this narrative, and before long, the money economy takes on a strangely fictitious quality and social reality seems to be borne into the clouds.

At some indeterminate point between the emergence of primordial barter and the development of high finance, traditional accounts bring the state into the picture. First, sovereign government places its authoritative stamp on our humble money token. Henceforth the state will oversee the minting of coin. Standardizing the production of coin and stabilizing its value, the sovereign is entitled to what is called "seigniorage," which is the profit derived from the difference between a coin's face and metal value. Next, the state enters into a social contract with the citizenry, pledging to regulate commerce, enforce property rights, and punish those who do not play by the rules. As part of this bargain, the state can provision the public sector by taxing or borrowing from private money holders. Still, because excessive taxation hampers productivity and overspending risks debauching a currency's value, according to orthodoxy, the state's role in a money economy is limited and best when practiced in moderation. Government may forge, shape, and enforce private exchange relations. It may assist the poor and tend to crises when something goes terribly wrong. When government promises a miracle, however, citizens should take cover. Such a promise is, standard accounts warn, a step toward tyranny or, worse, economic collapse.

The foregoing, of course, is a synthesis of several competing stories of modern money. It combines disparate and in certain respects incompatible Classical, Neoclassical, Austrian, Marxist, and mainstream Keynesian accounts within a single sweeping narrative. Between these divergent accounts, money's ontology wobbles and fractures then splits into seemingly incompatible and antagonistic forms. Here I do not dwell on their differences but rather sketch the relatively consistent image of money that crystallizes in the space where they coincide. Indeed, a series of more or less unquestioned assumptions links modernity's apparently irreconcilable approaches to money. These assumptions may be summarized as follows: (1) Money finds its immediate basis in an autonomous private exchange relation. (2) Money functions as an abstract representation, extension, and repository of finite value. (3) The modern system of production results from scaling up money's simple exchange relation into a complex system of private profit-making; (4) expanding networks of trade and finance make money circulate in increasingly broad patterns around the globe. (5) Finance subjects production to more abstract processes, which are divorced from yet still organize local material relations. (6) Governments come to regulate and enforce the money relation only subsequent to its development in autonomous market relations. And (7) governments remain constrained by limited capacities to tax and borrow and thus are forever beholden to the vicissitudes of the private sector.

To complicate matters, this orthodox conception of money is more often embraced as a useful fiction, not a historical fact. Adam Smith derived money from a "propensity to truck and barter."[6] Karl Marx, too, seemed to accept that monetary exchange develops out of simple exchange relations. When contemporary Neoclassicals, Austrians, Marxists, and mainstream Keynesians are pressed to speak on such matters, however, most admit that scant archaeological or historical evidence supports the exchange story. And yet, whether this story is adopted guilelessly, rejected outright, or accepted as a useful myth, the modern economic orthodoxy is retained in its basic structure and premises.[7] In this drama, private exchange is the hero and government, a tagalong sidekick. This sidekick may assist the hero. It may bring force when necessary. Still, government is noticeably ineffectual when it comes to driving the story. Though it may take part in the money relation, market exchange remains the economy's protagonist. Government is never the star of the show.

Marxism does not seriously challenge this orthodox story, but the virtue of its intervention is that it exposes the limits of the Liberal money relation as it is widely understood. In particular, Marxism points to how this money form undercuts the claims to universal egalitarianism promised by modern Liberal democracy. While Classical, Neoclassical, Austrian, and mainstream Keynesian economists variously affirm the money relation as a worthwhile and always salvageable social system, Marxism sees this system as built on a series of interlocking and ruinous contradictions. On one hand, Marxism understands money to be a private instrument that enables and naturalizes class domination, or the systemic exploitation of the many by the few. On the other hand, Marxism takes this systemic domination to be inherently uncontrollable, unstable, and destructive. This unwieldiness not only makes universal participation and well-being impossible but also undermines the capitalist class money is supposed to serve. Unlike adherents of Classical, Neoclassical, Austrian, and Keynesian economics, Marxists surmise that money cannot be made to support collective existence and that a just and truly egalitarian political project requires abandoning the money relation altogether.

Marxism traces both monetary domination and money's social unwieldiness to money's abstract basis. Specifically, it points to money's status as a mathematical equivalent. Most schools treat this equivalent as a neutral mediator of exchange between formally equal parties. Yet Marxism contends that monetary abstraction is the means by which a bourgeois-controlled marketplace institutionalizes unemployment and forces previously self-subsistent persons to sell their labor as equivalent commodities in order to survive. On such premises, the capitalist class extracts a phantom value from the working class that Marxism calls *Mehrwert*, or "surplus value."[8] Conceived as an intangible and yet socially determinative quantity that is generated in aggregate, surplus value is defined as the value created by wageworkers that exceeds capital costs and is appropriated by owners as profit. From this perspective, Marxism sees monetary abstraction as the source of collective dispossession, political mystification, and the tyranny of a minority over the majority.

At the same time, however, Marxism depicts monetary abstraction as a peripatetic, conflicting, and ultimately uncontrollable self-movement, or "automatic subject," which destabilizes the totality and, with it, bourgeois claims on power.[9] Money, on this reading, is a generalized movement of dispossession from which no capitalist is safe. In *Capital, Volume I*, Marx writes, "Because money is the metamorphosed shape of all other commodities, the result of their general alienation, for this reason it is alienable itself without restriction or condition."[10] On this view, monetary abstraction enables capitalists to squeeze surplus value from workers who have been subordinated to the wage relation. It also represents the unrestricted alienation of value that drives commodity production in a modern money economy. It is precisely this unconditioned and limitless alienability, meanwhile, that undermines the owning class and sends the entire system into a series of crises.

Most destabilizing among these crises is the tendency of the overall profit rate to fall.[11] In this case, individual firms and entrepreneurs make short-term profits in a money economy, but the rate of profit declines as a whole. This aggregate evacuation of value sets off a chain of reactions and compensatory mechanisms that spread loss and instability throughout the economy. Falling profits threaten capitalists with expulsion from the owning class. Such downward pressure promotes a race to the bottom in the market. Owners further exploit workers, reduce wages, and cut benefits while investing in new capital and seeking fresh markets to keep both themselves and the economy afloat. When these efforts fail, Marxists warn, capitalists borrow more money and turn to speculative financial instruments to generate so-called "fictitious capital," which tends to exceed the production of tangible assets.[12] The results are uncontrollable financial bubbles that periodically crash and destabilize the entire economic order.

On my analysis, the Marxist critique of political economy is revelatory, but the foundations of its critique are spurious. In tracing the Liberal money form's tendency toward loss and crises, Marxism unwittingly reveals something crucial about its basic metaphysical structure. Yet it fails to suggest that money might appear differently than Liberal modernity has imagined. As I argued in my introduction and will develop in later chapters, Marxist analysis insists that the Liberal money form takes the shape of a fleeting *thisness*, or *haecceity*, an abstraction that paradoxically behaves like a finite and disposable thing. The Liberal orthodoxy will affirm money's thisness, viewing it as a self-maintaining relation that facilitates a "mutual coincidence of wants."[13] Marxism challenges this coincidence, underscoring Liberal money's topological non-coincidence, which never sufficiently provides for everyone in all places at all times. Marxism does not appeal explicitly to the language of haecceity, of course. Instead, it implies, connotes, and metaphorizes this haecceity by imagining money ceaselessly forging and dissolving spatial arrangements as it courses in and out of particular locales. On this view, money shuttles here when it is needed there and seems to be dizzyingly nowhere and everywhere at once.

Marxism presents a powerful critique of social domination. However, it is this school's revelations about the Liberal money form's haecceity and tendency toward loss that most distinguish Marxism from the rest of modern economic thought. Frequently overshadowed by denunciations of class power and exploitation, Marxism's understanding of the Liberal money form's systemic hemorrhaging of value represents its most important contribution to modern political economy. With it, Marxism shows that Liberal money is essentially *unanswerable* because it systemically eludes social capture. Liberal money flees, scatters, and dissolves, yielding to no logic or agency other than its own. It amplifies productive capacities and expands the scale of social relations. Yet it also depoliticizes the money form, which remains structurally incapable of being seized and organized toward deliberate political ends.

By revealing the political unanswerability of the Liberal money form, Marxism indicates the fatal defect at the heart of the modern democratic state: its dependence upon Liberal money's fugitive thisness. Governments have struggled with this merciless money form throughout the modern period. It is, in fact, an almost universally accepted maxim of modern historians that powerful governments collapse when they become excessively indebted to private lenders, since fiscal crises open the door to revolutions. The overextended regime of Louis XVI, for instance, occasioned not only compensatory tax hikes but also the historic meeting of the Estates General and the French Revolution that followed it. Russia's February Revolution and October Revolution are similarly attributed to Tsar Nicholas II's disastrous mishandling of the economy. Having devoted exorbitant funds to the Great War, he decided to make vodka illegal. The result curtailed tax revenues that supported expenditures to curb domestic unemployment and food shortages. With soldiers dying on the front and workers and peasants starving at home, the Romanov regime quickly folded, as did the provisional bourgeois government that replaced the tsar. As a consequence, Bolsheviks seized the state with relative ease.

Liberal money thwarts modern governments in more common ways, too, unsettling quotidian bureaucratic operations. In general the state is understood to steer between the Scylla of recession-inducing taxes and the Charybdis of hyperinflationary overspending. This seemingly impossible task regularly leaves a sizable portion of the population unemployed. Assessing a nineteenth century defined by cruel labor practices and crisis-ridden financial markets, Marx and Friedrich Engels called this group of systemically excluded workers an "unemployed reserve army."[14] Their argument was not merely that monetary economies tend to condemn people to unemployment and destitution. It was also that as a pool of laborers willing to work in desperate conditions and for little pay, the reserve army of the unemployed play a debilitating role in a money economy that erodes the stability of the system from below. Hampering labor's bargaining power and advancing capitalist exploitation, this army rattles the social order with civil unrest and revolutionary uprisings. It is Liberal money's most definitive symptom and the greatest liability for the operation and survival of the modern state.

In the United States the so-called "New Deal Order" sought to contain these forces with progressive taxation, capital controls, welfare programs, counter-cyclical deficit spending, and a massive military industrial complex. Even in the midst of this high-growth "Goldilocks economy," however, unemployment remained at depression levels in the African American community, and calls for publicly funded black employment were met with cries of inflation. According to a certain version of late twentieth-century history, spending on the Vietnam War and union-led wage gains eventually led to a low-growth inflationary spiral during the late 1960s and throughout the 1970s. Promising to "Whip Inflation Now," the Ford and later Carter administrations tightened fiscal policy, and Federal Reserve Chair Paul Volcker jacked up interest rates well into the 1980s, causing a sharp deflationary contraction and pushing the unemployment rate above 10 percent at its peak.[15]

The subsequent neoliberal onslaught of destabilizing finance, global competition, and union busting proved the lie of the Liberal money form, which cannot answer to politics or tame its crisis-inducing contradictions. To make matters worse, the demise of the Soviet Union and its inflexible command economy makes a return to the welfare state seem the only legible alternative. Such a return would no doubt improve present circumstances. But it is hardly a foundation for critical theory or a *telos* for politics. After all, a decade after the 2007–2008 global financial crisis, we now face regular un- and underemployment, real-wage stagnation; punishing austerity; stunted production; predatory finance; destabilizing speculation; capital flight; tax havens; exploitative global supply chains; dead-end service work; unbearable private debts; unaffordable child, health, and elder care; insufficient housing; militarized policing; mass incarceration; immigration crises; factory farming; deforestation; collapsing ecosystems; global warming; and superstorms. Marxism makes clear that the Liberal money form is wholly inadequate for addressing neoliberalism's social and ecological catastrophes. It suggests that critical theory can neither take this money relation as given nor aim merely to repair it. Yet, if the Left wishes to abandon this money form and seize hold of collective governance, then it must move beyond Marxist critiques of the Liberal money relation, which only undermine sustained collective transformation.

The Liberal money form's tendency to impede and forfeit modern egalitarian revolutions makes the requirement to move beyond Marxist criticism more vivid. From French to Bolshevik revolutions, debacles involving crushing public debts, over- and under-taxation, and run-away inflation crippled experiments in radical egalitarian governance.[16] Economic chaos and insecurity ushered violent and oppressive political regimes into power, those of Napoleon Bonaparte and Joseph Stalin being prime examples. Because private exchange fundamentally alienates social labor and eludes collective capture, says Marxism, true justice remains impossible in a world organized by money. As long as the money medium continues to condition social production, history seems to tell us, even radically egalitarian governments are likely to give way to the shifting winds of world commerce. And yet to equip ourselves only with the Marxist critique of money without envisioning a contrary way forward means continuing to suffer neoliberalism's interminable twilight with no inkling of a genuine alternative.

Aesthetic Appeals

In the face of Liberal money's limits, modern society has sought redemption in the aesthetic domain. With the aesthetic, the modern bourgeois class imagined that freer, more diverse, and more replete logics of sense and belonging could fill the migrating lack at the center of economic life. To do so, the bourgeoisie initially separated the aesthetic sphere from its traditional institutions and rituals as a refuge from monetized relations. Concerns with matters of sensibility, taste, culture, and art established a space of autonomy and protection, where the bourgeois class could escape the reckless sway of the market without actually seeking to overcome it. The aesthetic enriched experience. It expanded the senses. It fostered communal feelings squelched by commercial life and plunged subjects into the as yet unimagined and unknown.

Perhaps above all, the aesthetic provided the sort of *answerability* that is missing from the money relation and the world it organizes. In its modern formulation, the aesthetic implies intentionality, deliberation, and concerted effort. It presumes that persons still act as authors of worldly relations and that someone, somewhere, is responsible. The contemporary German art critic Diedrich Diedrichsen offers a rather cynical account of this operation that nevertheless manages to put the social stakes of the aesthetic's answerability into sharp relief: "Art clings to society or life or systems suspected of being meaningless and contingent, and then in the end, it suddenly comes up with an originator who is responsible for the whole mess. That is sufficient consolation for even the harshest poetry of hopelessness and negation: the fact that there is someone who wrote it down."[17] Aesthetic production promises intentionality and responsibility in the face of a modernity that appears arbitrary and heedless. It does so, Diedrichsen implies, by creating what might be called a *locus of accountability* that, beyond particular affirmations or negations, becomes a site of reckoning for a world without such things.

In this way, the aesthetic redresses the primal scene with which the orthodox story of Liberal money begins: the moment when embodied social actors enter into an exchange relation. In this immediate exchange situation, money involves a precarious transfer of value that seems to alienate social life from the start. The aesthetic strives to circumvent this alienation by creating a replete, multifarious, and open mode of social production that is responsive to violence, exploitation, and suffering. The aesthetic's challenge, in other words, is to resist money's hemorrhaging thisness and experiment with forms of life that are not predicated upon privation.

Given the aesthetic's response to the Liberal money form, it is unsurprising that socialists, communists, and anarchists embraced the aesthetic as an ideal model for political emancipation during the nineteenth century. Twentieth-century critical theorists, too, looked to the aporias and possibilities of the aesthetic as points of departure from the scientism of Second International Marxism. Whereas early theorists conceived this project as a weak force against monetary alienation, late twentieth-century thinkers found that the market had subsumed the aesthetic and destroyed the dialectical opposition between money and aesthetics. Since that time, postmodern or contemporary aesthetics has adopted many of the utopian problems and impulses that animated their modern predecessors. Yet unlike modern aesthetics, the contemporary project accedes to the Liberal money form's historical triumph and pursues the aesthetic's sensuousness, diversity, and communality *from the point of view* of this dialectical collapse.

Affective and philosophical positions differ wildly in the aesthetic's contemporary resurrection. Some aestheticians continue to insist upon the aesthetic's minimal autonomy from the realm of capitalist competition and reckless finance.[18] Others walk back the date of the collapse of money and aesthetics, often affirming Adorno's earlier dialectical assertion that aesthetic autonomy was illusory from the start.[19] Another dominant strain of thought concedes the failure of the aesthetic project but mobilizes its terms to do battle with a hyperaestheticized marketplace.[20] Still others affirm the surfeit sensuousness, diversity, and communality of neoliberal aesthetics, which, they argue, manage to exceed political repression and commercial capture.[21] A final approach doubles down on the Liberal money form itself, aestheticizing peer-to-peer currencies and abstract financial instruments or advocating the embrace of riot, disaster, and social collapse.[22] Regardless, no serious writer or artist openly celebrates the aesthetic's flat subservience to neoliberalism's so-called creative economy.[23] No one denies that the aesthetic project has reached something of a historical impasse. Indeed, even avid multiculturalists and fervent accelerationists know that pursuing the aesthetic today means working against a sense of epochal exhaustion.

The French artist and erstwhile critic Claire Fontaine captures the tenor of this exhaustion in a piece titled "Our Common Critical Condition." The essay is worth quoting at length:

Life is no longer something we all share, something in which we all accompany one another, but an individualized affair of accumulation, labor, and self-affirmation. We live like this with no hope for political change (however necessary) in our lives, nor a common language capable of naming this need or allowing us to define together what is particular to our present. This condition is new, no doubt unique in Western history; it is so painful and engenders such a profound solitude and loss of dignity that we sometimes catch ourselves doubting the sincerity of artworks that are created under such conditions—for we know that their fate is uncertain, and will most likely disappoint. Nevertheless, the field of art has never been so free, vast, and attractive to the general public—and this is perhaps precisely what makes our present condition a profoundly critical one.[24]

Fontaine links the political limits of Liberal money to the aesthetic's historical impasse. Economic life under neoliberalism has made aesthetic production hyperindividualist, consumerist, and transient. The result infuses the aesthetic with uncertainty and political hopelessness. There is no shared language for responding to present disorder in concert. Yet Fontaine admits that aesthetic creation has never seemed so accessible, expansive, and appealing. With this, she performs what she previously deemed impossible: she "give[s] a name" to "our common critical condition" in a way that might foment a shared political project. Still, the essay's tone is overwhelmingly weary, which casts doubt on the prospects for this work. In fact, if Fontaine is correct in designating the critical condition of the aesthetic in our time, then this condition lacks historical directionality and dialectical force.

In what follows I chart an alternative course for the dialectic between money and aesthetics. To push forward, I argue, it is crucial to loop back. We must reimagine and wholly rearticulate the primal scene that structures the historical antagonism between money and aesthetics. We must dissolve the dialectical impetus that leads to today's neoliberal dead-end. My wager is that MMT provides the critical leverage for carrying this out. As a boundless public center, MMT's counter-image of money refuses the originary privation that structures the money/aesthetics dialectic. It replaces the Liberal politics of privation with a contest over money's essential infinitude, publicness, and answerability. It eradicates the social need for an aesthetic sphere that is external and/or opposed to the medium that organizes social production in general. MMT thus furnishes a more capacious and more practicable vehicle for redeeming what Adorno lamentingly deemed modernity's "damaged life."[25] It renews the saving powers of money and the aesthetic legacy we have inherited. More profoundly, it permits us to transcend the aesthetic as previously imagined.

Creature of the State

MMT fundamentally reconfigures the orthodox story of money and the metaphysics it implies. Though MMT does not speak the language of metaphysics, it assumes a social topology and causal order wholly incompatible with Liberal money. It refuses to predicate problems of political economy on what I have called the alienating haecceity of the original cell of exchange. Instead, MMT begins from the presumption that money arises from a financially unconstrained political center. It asks how governing this primary infinitude actively constructs the economic totality from beginning to end. Such is the key for grasping MMT's originality and for distinguishing it from Classical, Neoclassical, Marxist, Austrian, and Keynesian economics. These schools debate how government can or should add to what is a private and finite economic field. MMT instead demonstrates how the public sector comprises the causal center of economic activity. Every monetary relation is but a finite realization of an infinite public balance sheet. With this, MMT makes money, rather than capital, the prime mover of political economy. It replaces Liberal money's fugitive thisness with an inalienable public medium that is always already there. This medium can be distributed, therefore, everywhere that money is needed.

A cursory survey of MMT's origins clarifies both its debts to previous theories and its historical exceptionality. Specifically, MMT is indebted to two overlapping genealogies that comprise what the late economist Fred Lee has called the "heterodox" tradition of political economy: chartalism and Keynesianism. One finds historical precedents for the chartalist tradition in the nineteenth-century British Banking School, the American monetary radicalism of Edward Kellogg, and passing claims by the Classical political economy of Adam Smith and David Ricardo.[26] The term *chartalism* was coined, however, by an early twentieth-century scholar of the German Historical School, Georg Friedrich Knapp. Knapp had been a great admirer of Georg Simmel's philosophical sociology and, in particular, the latter's complex figuration of money as embodying the pure contingency and flux of modern urban life. But in his own published work, Knapp developed a more technical, juridical analysis of money that implicitly broke with the metaphysics of exchange underwriting Simmel's understanding of money as contingent fluctuations.

In his primary work, *The State Theory of Money* (1905), Knapp argues that money originates through neither private exchange relations founded on individual faith nor valuable commodities such as precious metals. Instead, he regards money as a "creature of law" and a creation of the state.[27] A money economy comes into being, first, when a government defines an abstract unit of account, and second, when that government accepts representatives of this abstract unit as legal means of payment. Knapp thus detaches money's ontology from what he calls "autometallist" conceptions of private commodity exchange. He also roots money's social function and value entirely in juridical and political domains.

Read by few and not widely accepted, Knapp's book was followed by the chartalist writings of English diplomat Alfred Mitchell Innes. Mitchell Innes was unfamiliar with Knapp's *The State Theory of Money*, which would not be translated into English until 1924. Yet in two short and largely ignored papers titled "What Is Money?" and "The Credit Theory of Money," published in the *Banking Law Journal* in 1913 and 1914, respectively, Mitchell Innes emphasizes money's political and juridical foundations not unlike Knapp.[28] He similarly claims that money is a relation comprising abstract credits and debts that remains irreducible to the money-things that have historically represented it. Mitchell Innes goes further than Knapp, too, stipulating the part that taxation plays in forging and maintaining a money economy. Tracing the origins of money to a complex system of tribal fines designed to settle communal feuds, Knapp argues that a polity establishes a money system by levying a tax obligation in a unit it defines and furnishes. Contrary to the dominant view, Mitchell Innes stresses not the revenue function of the tax but rather its role in creating the demand for a currency in the first place. Enforcing a tax compels people to labor to earn state currency so as to avoid sanction by community authorities. From this angle, taxation resembles a form of punishment and potential violence that is immediately tied to structures of political power. From another perspective, however—one Mitchell Innes leaves underdeveloped—the tax socializes labor by enforcing a debt to the state that impels persons to work together in order to meet public obligations.

Neither Knapp nor Mitchell Innes is primarily concerned with debates about metal standards and their limiting effects on banking and commerce. Neither speaks directly to what the state or credit theory of money means for government finance and fiscal policy. Yet by expressly desubstantializing and politicizing money's social ontology, these early twentieth-century chartalists opened the door for John Maynard Keynes. Keynes read and cited both Knapp and Mitchell Innes early in his career, referring to these youthful preoccupations with money's ontology and origins as a period of "Babylonian madness."[29] In his *A Treatise on Money* (1930), meanwhile, Keynes proposes a semiotics of the monetary relation that is firmly anchored in governmental authority:

> The State, therefore, comes in first of all as the authority of law which enforces the payment of the thing which corresponds to the name or description in the contract. But it comes in doubly when, in addition, it claims the right to determine and declare what thing corresponds to the name, and to vary its declaration from time to time—when, that is to say, it claims the right to re-edit the dictionary. This right is claimed by all modern States and has been so claimed for some four thousand years at least. It is when this stage in the evolution of Money has been reached that Knapp's Chartalism—the doctrine that money is peculiarly a creation of the State—is fully realized. . . . Today all civilized money is, beyond the possibility of dispute, chartalist.[30]

Keynes pushes back against the barter mythology that guides Neoclassical economist Alfred Marshall and his nineteenth-century faith in utility maximization and the self-regulating laws of supply and demand. In place of Marshall's laissez-faire approach, Keynes argues that money is indisputably chartalist and has been for at least 4,000 years. Its function as measure, meaning, and value derives first and foremost from state author-ity. The primary "law" that regulates the money relation is that which is legislated and enforced by human governments. Moreover, governments hold the power to transform money's semiotic status, a capacity that Keynes compares to a "right to re-edit the dictionary."

In both *A Treatise on Money* and, later, *The General Theory of Employment, Interest and Money* (1936), Keynes mobilizes Knapp's and Mitchell Innes's chartalist insights to underscore the failure of laissez-faire principles. Against these principles Keynes granted fiscal policy a greater role in stabilizing an inherently unstable commercial sphere.[31] Keynes also challenged the paradoxical Neoclassical assumption that markets tend toward full employment while maintaining a natural rate of unemployment that prevents inflation. By contrast, Keynes asserts that full employment comes from the state, not the market. There is no tradeoff, moreover, between employment and price stability. To achieve full employment, governments should borrow and spend enough to make up for insufficient private sector spending but not so much that it leads to inflationary overheating. Keynes spurns the ideology of so-called sound finance and its strict adherence to balancing government budgets. With strong and consistent counter-cyclical fiscal borrowing and spending, he concludes, a state can assist in cultivating full employment and a prosperous economy while at the same time paying debtors through taxes levied on the resulting productivity. Keynes also argues that inflation is not the imminent threat against which Neoclassical theorists warned. Rather, prices tend not to fluctuate rapidly and persistently in a fully functioning economy. Set by large firms, they are frequently driven downward by inter-firm competition. Wage rates rise and fall, meanwhile, with slow and ongoing struggles between capital and labor. For these reasons, prices do not show a propensity to change quickly, and a well-allocated fiscal stimulus is unlikely to produce inflation, according to Keynes.

That said, Keynes remains cautious when it comes to fiscal spending, maintaining that governments should mind their debts and that budgets ought to be balanced over the course of a business cycle. In this sense Keynes paves the way for what I have referred to as "mainstream" American Keynesianism, the economic theory that would become associated with a robust military industrial complex and expanded welfare state. Emblematized by Paul Samuelson's epoch-defining textbook *Economics*

(1948), American Keynesianism was based on a deliberately conservative reading of Keynes that claimed to synthesize the English economist's work with the Neoclassical free-market tradition from which it departed. This Keynesian-Neoclassical synthesis justified a midcentury expansion of the public sector and a hearty program of fiscal stimulus and counter-cyclical spending fueled by government borrowing. However, it also affirmed the efficiency of markets, preferred supply-side tax cuts to targeted fiscal policy, embraced a natural rate of unemployment, and demanded that state budgets be balanced over the business cycle. This, along with white, patriarchal, heteronormative politics, left a sizable portion of the population unemployed, exploited, and unprotected.

Meanwhile, chartalism underwent a seismic shift in the hands of post-Keynesian market socialists Michal Kalecki, Hyman Minsky, and Abba Lerner.[32] Kalecki, Minsky, and Lerner emerged from the more radical and Marxist impulses that animated the early "post-" or "Cambridge Keynesians," a group that included economists such as Joan Robinson, Nicholas Kaldor, Paul Davidson, and Piero Sraffa. European émigrés working in the United States, Kalecki, Minsky, and Lerner eschewed the imperative to balance government budgets over the business cycle and rejected fears of hyperinflation as unwarranted. They also dislodged the keystones that held the Liberal monetary order together: (1) states must tax or borrow before spending, and (2) governments are somehow fiscally constrained by nature. The only limits to state spending, they asserted, are the finite persons, materials, and productive capacities that are available for fiscal policy to mobilize at a given moment. The sole obstacle to true full employment is not financial, writes Kalecki, but political.[33] To wit, he, Minsky, and Lerner foreground money's chartal constitution as a limitless public instrument while critiquing Soviet-style planning, which aims, they argue, to formulate and organize all economic activity directly from that political center. Instead, they advocate a fiscal program oriented toward true full employment that is based on Keynes's own notion of the state as an Employer of Last Resort. On this model, government hires every willing and able person who cannot find meaningful work in the private sector, essentially ensuring that there are always more positions available than persons seeking jobs.[34]

Writing amid anticommunist witch hunts and a nightmarish Jim Crow South, Kalecki, Minsky, and Lerner were no doubt aware of both the political and epistemic implications of their chartalist contentions and recommendations. To insist that full employment is a matter of political will, not affordability, is a radical claim, regardless of how underdeveloped its consequences in their own work might have been. Such a system would rapidly eliminate poverty and the ills that accompany it. It would abolish the reserve army of unemployed citizens willing to work below market rates. It would undercut capital's exploitation of labor, increase workers' political power, and, if genuinely universal, integrate African Americans and other racial and ethnic groups into American society with dignity. Indeed, because one may read such transformations between the lines of the work by Kalecki, Minsky, and Lerner, it is no surprise to discover that they were frequently policed, marginalized, and repressed within the academy and in policy circles.

To grasp the unnerving epistemic rupture this chartalism represented, we need only turn to Keynes's own ambivalent relations with Lerner. Keynes wavered anxiously in his support of "Functional Finance," Lerner's theory of unrestricted fiscal policy. "The central idea [of Functional Finance]," writes Lerner, "is that government fiscal policy, its spending and taxing, its borrowing and repayment of loans, its issue of new money and its withdrawal of money, shall all be undertaken with an eye only to the *results* of these actions on the economy and not to any established traditional doctrine about what is sound or unsound."[35] In contradiction to the arbitrary economic laws and damaging debt limits of sound finance, Functional Finance judges fiscal and monetary policies primarily by their public purpose and social effects. In the broadest sense, this means ensuring full employment and price stability.

Keynes initially denounced Functional Finance, calling its utter rejection of sound budgeting over the business cycle "humbug."[36] He increasingly warmed to Lerner's proposition, however, softening his resistance to Functional Finance and declaring its underlying logic sound. In 1944 Keynes wrote to Lerner congratulating him on the recent publication of *The Economics of Control*. In his letter Keynes toys with the idea of acquainting various heads of treasuries with the principles of Functional Finance, reflecting somewhat humorously on the difficulty and likely impossibility of Lerner's ideas being accepted.

> It is very original and grand stuff. I shall have to try when I get back to hold a seminar for the heads of the Treasury on Functional Finance. It will be very hard going—probably impossible. I shall have to temper its austerity where I can. I think I shall ask them to let me hold a seminar of their sons instead, agreeing beforehand that, if I can convince the boys, they will take it from me that it is so![37]

Here Keynes flexes his characteristic wit and political acumen. What begins as an expression of support for Functional Finance quickly devolves into an oblique admission that the world is neither epistemologically nor politically prepared to receive, let alone comprehend, Lerner's perspective. "His argument is impeccable," Keynes reflects in a separate letter to economist James Meade. "But heaven help anyone who tries to put it across (to) the plain man at this present state of the evolution of our ideas."[38]

Hoping to cut through such irony-infused hedging, Lerner purportedly put the matter to Keynes at a dinner following a Federal Reserve Board meeting in 1945. Economist David Colander describes the scene as follows:

> Lerner approached Keynes and asked: "Mr. Keynes, why don't we forget all this business of fiscal policy, public debt and all those things, and have some printing presses." Keynes, after looking around the room to see that no newspaper reporters could hear, replied: "It's the art of statesmanship to tell lies but they must be plausible lies."[39]

However apocryphal, Keynes's response to Lerner registers the gravitas of midcentury chartalism's challenge to the Liberal money form. The post-Keynesian chartalism of Kalecki, Minsky, and Lerner befuddles the opposition between truth and lie that persons in power habitually transgress and exploit. Chartalism may be logically coherent and persuasively argued, but on Keynes's admission, it exceeds "plausibility." Surpassing the realm of intelligibility, it requires the assistance of "heaven" to penetrate our secular reality.

Modern Monetary Theory, or the Politics of Redemption

Though mainstream Keynesianism dismissed chartalism, it quietly persevered Chicago School Monetarism and Mont Pelerin neoliberalism, reemerging in the 1990s amid debates about the "endogenous," as opposed to "exogenous," theory of money creation.[40] The exogenous theory, held by orthodox economists, treats money as an extant quantity that can be variously recycled, expanded, or contracted. On this view, banks require deposits before they can loan money to private investors, and banking is thought to operate by loaning out their reserve holdings. In endogenous theory, banks are also responsible for modulating aggregate quantities of money, but they do not depend on finite reserve deposits. Instead, they create money out of thin air every time they authorize a new loan. Loans thus precede deposits, and external or exogenous institutions such as central banks have little effect on the total amount of money in circulation. Often called the "circuitist" approach, endogenous theory emphasizes money's institutional circuits in place of falsely substantializing visions of what is uncritically referred to as the "money supply."

From this marginalized milieu arose a neochartalist project that came to be dubbed Modern Monetary Theory. In a sense, MMT forges a synthesis of previous insights: Knapp's state theory; Mitchell Innes's tax-driven money; Keynes's fiscal chartalism; post-Keynesian chartalism's unapologetically limitless fiscal instrument; and the endogenous theory of money creation. MMT does more than amalgamate former views, however; it also supplies an absolute shift in perspective by presenting a positive vision of the totality. MMT thus reconceives money's basic topology and rethinks the causal structure of political economy.

Still, MMT economists often fail to make their intervention explicit. To compensate for their failure to do so, let me describe their project as follows: MMT envisions money as a boundless public center and imagines this center as the prime mover upon which all particular economic relations depend. MMT, then, corroborates yet challenges former chartalist positions. It, too, grounds money in state law and liberates government's fiscal capacities. Unlike its predecessors, however, MMT does not consign money to particular expenditures that tie currency to a metaphysics of thisness, or haecceity. Instead, it places money's universality behind its particularity and installs infinitude within finite transactions. As a result, political economy no longer asks how governments might assist and regulate markets; it asks how a boundless public utility conditions each and every economic relation from the start.

MMT formed during the 1990s, when the American post-Keynesian chartalists L. Randall Wray, Stephanie Kelton, and Mathew Forstater met the Australian Kaleckian Marxist Bill Mitchell and then joined forces with American hedge fund manager Warren Mosler. Never trained as an economist, Mosler was largely unacquainted with both the history of economic thought and its contemporary literature. Yet, Mosler offered this group of post-Keynesian chartalists a novel and quite singular way of framing the basic presuppositions and problems of political economy.[41]

Moser's key insight is this: government spending is never a borrowing operation, even when it seems to involve selling treasury securities to the private sector.[42] Public expenditure begins when the legislature gives legal authorization for spending. Next, the central bank disperses money to fund the expenditures in question. Only then does the treasury sell interest-bearing bonds to private bidders. The government always spends before it seems to borrow, in other words. Moreover, Mosler shows that what appears to be government borrowing is, in fact, a way for the state to manage and direct economic activity politically under the cloak of economic necessity.

Instead of financing public spending, Mosler argues, bond sales coordinate relations among large banks and set the conditions for everything from private debt levels and rates of productive investment to employment and poverty. Above all, bond sales decrease the level of liquidity in the banking system. Mosler calls this lessening of available funds a "reserve drain" operation and shows how keeping money dear allows government to push what is called the "Overnight Rate" above zero.[43] As the interest rate large banks charge when lending to one another, the Overnight Rate serves as a barometer for all other interest rates in the economy. The official reason given for maintaining the Overnight Rate above zero is that it suppresses harmful inflationary pressures. But in practice, an above-zero Overnight Rate increases private debt and diminishes productive investment while raising unemployment and exacerbating poverty along classed, gendered, and racialized lines. That is why Mosler and other MMT economists will insist that the so-called natural rate of interest is always zero.[44]

Joining bond sales to public spending is not only socially damaging, according to Mosler, but also misleading, contradictory, and confused. It makes government's fiscal capacity appear like that of a cash-strapped firm; it perpetuates the myth of an autonomous central bank that is unaccountable to the legislature authorizing its activities; and it naturalizes destructive above-zero interest rates that contract productive investment and increase the miseries of un- and underemployment. What seems like government borrowing is, in truth, a state-sanctioned process furnishing wealthy elites with risk-free, interest-earning assets that give them more money than they would otherwise earn. But the decreases in gross domestic product that result from high interest rates undercut the value of a currency and lessen the wealthy's purchasing power, while stoking financial instability and social conflict.

No doubt such a self-destructive system may be explained by appealing to the notion of the "death drive," Freud's speculative term for a self-annihilating impulse that is supposed to undercut straightforward instincts toward preservation. I address this matter more directly in chapter 2. For the time being, I wish to remark only that naked class interest cannot alone account for the self-sabotaging operations that underlie the feint of government borrowing.

To make things still more paradoxical, the same wealthy classes that seem to profit from government bond sales decry their precarious gains every time they denounce a mounting public debt. As Mosler reveals, however, public debts are merely interest-bearing and generally unproductive securities held by the wealthy. Government can always meet monetary obligations when they come due. What is genuinely hazardous, meanwhile, is not public but rather private debt, particularly in the midst of diminishing productivity, employment, and aggregate spending power. These are the ingredients for vicious boom-and-bust cycles, painful recessions, and depressions. To tether bond sales to public spending is to obscure the mechanisms that produce such dangers. It is also to confront systemic economic difficulties from a muddled and self-destructive perspective.

In this light, Mosler's intervention completes what earlier chartalists initiated. It wholly desubstantializes the money relation by revealing that governments never borrow in currencies they alone generate. Mosler thus shifts the critique of political economy away from money's concrete finitude and toward its abstract and infinite universality. To be sure, chartalists from Knapp to Abba Lerner conceived money as an abstract credit relation grounded in state law. They also posited a government that does not need private sector money before it can spend. Yet Mosler and MMT go further. The state, he argues, never borrows in its own currency, and public spending always precedes any perceived borrowing. From this point of view, governments do not gain or lose money, rendering the language of possession and dispossession not only deceptive but also nonsensical. "The federal government neither has nor doesn't have dollars," writes Mosler.[45] Money is not an alienable entity governments amass or hemorrhage. It is a limitless writing instrument for mobilizing social production and provisioning the public purpose. It is, finally, the boundless public center from which any critique of political economy must begin.

This is the case, moreover, because money's inalienable universality conditions every economic relation. Abstract yet publicly accountable, money expresses a political obligation, according to Mosler, Wray, Kelton, and other MMT adherents, for which government is always responsible. When currency-issuing governments implement taxes, they impel citizens to participate in social labor to meet their obligations. In turn, governments are reciprocally compelled to ensure rightful access to this common store of wealth. For MMT, this obligation constitutes the money relation, not Liberalism's primal scene of exchange. Unlike the fugitive thisness of Liberal money, which is by turns present then absent or here then there, MMT's vision of money is always already ready to address all needs at all times.

MMT thus inverts the causal efficacy attributed to haecceity in Liberal theories of the money relation. It also challenges Marxism's unwitting naturalization of these same metaphysics. In fact, compared to MMT, Marxist critiques of political economy inadvertently reify the alienable and unanswerable thisness of Liberal money. Emphasizing the evacuation of money-things from persons or communities, Marxist theories of the money relation also denounce extractions of surplus value from the material conditions of labor and demand redistributions of finite wealth through taxation. To be sure, one should provide labor and access to all money users as well as control differentials between wages and profits or wealthy and poor. But to underscore evacuation and extraction in addition to redistribution is to sustain the haecceity of Liberal money and the fantastical play of presence and absence upon which its unanswerability turns.

MMT shares Marxism's goals of achieving an inclusive, egalitarian, and flourishing society in which everyone participates in meaningful activities, labor never licenses domination, and no one is left out in the cold. But MMT aims to achieve such a reality by affirming money's unrestricted public capacities, while dispensing with Liberal money's metaphysics of haecceity. Importantly, this means rebuffing what Wray calls the

"Robin Hood" approach to wealth creation and distribution: taxing the rich to give to the poor.[46] Instead, MMT advocates a political and legal system that supports social production and uses taxation and other measures to preclude wealth accumulation. As Wray puts it:

> Modern Money Theory is not against taxing the rich. Impose the highest tax you possibly can on the rich. We completely support that. We would go much further than that: don't let them earn the money in the first place. Make the kinds of activities that are enriching them illegal. If they are now breaking laws or they break future laws, throw them in jail. Confiscate all of their wealth. What we oppose is the argument that we need taxes on the rich to pay for the poor. Any sovereign government can pay for the poor without taxes.[47]

Wray severs the politics of public spending from traditional Robin Hood Leftism. Taxation is a political instrument for "pre-distributing" money, he argues, not a "redistribution" mechanism for recycling finite profits. Indeed, because the tax obligation legally grounds and maintains a monetary system, it may be used to control wealth inequality and gross disparities in political power. It may also be used to temper inflationary pressures when an economy reaches full employment and can no longer absorb additional public spending. In fact, the true object of contestation is fiscal policy, according to Wray. When one treats money as a finite quantity that must be wrested from capital, one obscures this lesson and forfeits a public utility to private interests. A Left that pursues money's fleeting thisness remains ensnared in an unresolvable and self-defeating game of cat-and-mouse in which the cat never realizes she is chasing her own tail.

MMT, by contrast, traces the money relation's concentric spirals through time. Here money issues from the center as state-issued debt. This debt is a public IOU, or promise to pay, authorized by a central bank or treasury. Circulating IOUs are then mobilized for productive purposes and deferred toward later ends. Still, for such debts to be realized qua money, government perpetually needs to ensure their legal acceptability. Public authority must iteratively make good on past promises. There is, in other words, perpetual redemption at the center of money's spiraling temporality. When it fails or is obscured and repressed, the social and ecological totality suffers. We might say, therefore, that monetary politics are a politics of redemption. "Creation must precede Redemption," writes Wray. "Those who think a sovereign must first get tax revenue before spending, . . . who believe a central bank must first obtain reserves before lending them, . . . who believe a private bank must first obtain deposits before lending them . . . have all confused Redemption with Creation. . . . Receipt of taxes, receipt of reserve deposits, and receipt of demand deposits are all Acts of Redemption."[48]

Some MMT scholars have thematized money's historical intertwinements with religion. But these treatments rhetorically distance themselves from money's religious foundations and prefer sociological sobriety to exploring money's social and theological potentiality. If, however, we are to realize what MMT reveals about money's obfuscated political structure and social potential, then it is necessary, I argue, to take such "metaphysical subtleties and theological niceties" seriously and embrace what critical political economy has historically derided, overlooked, or leveraged against the money relation.[49] To overcome neoliberal destruction and suffering, we must dive headlong into the riddling structure of our present indebtedness. We must rejoice in money's boundless capacities for redemption. We must shift the locus of critical theory from the aesthetic relation to the money relation. Only then may we transcend the modern aesthetic project as it has been historically articulated and experienced.

2
Declarations of Dependence

Political power is not comparable to the category of energy in
physics. Nor is power the sole category of political science. . . .
The trend to equate politics with power politics goes back to
Machiavelli and appears to have become the predominant trait of
American and, perhaps, of modern political science in general.
—Franz L. Neumann

Center: from kentein, *"stitch,"* kenteo, *"to prick," denotes (a) "a*
sting," Rev. 9:10; metaphorically, of sin as the "sting" of death, 1 Cor.
15:55, 56; (b) "a goad," Acts. 26:14; "pricks," said of the promptings
and misgivings which Saul of Tarsus had resisted before conversion.
—Anonymous

The problem of the political is irreducible to a field of power.
After all, the modern category of the political derives from the
ancient Greek *polis*. A centrally organized city-state, the polis
was not only ruled by political elites but also cultivated and
sustained by enduring public institutions. To persist, it had to
entangle its members in the riddles and anxieties of collective
maintenance, or *care*, as much as in the questions of coercion,
subordination, and force that preoccupy most thinkers today.

In fact, premodern thought candidly confronted this *mystery of care*. From Athenian philosophy to late medieval theology, care was generally understood to be an inescapable social burden and the locus of cultivation and spiritual uplift. Conceived as such, the problems of care were included squarely within the domain of the political and informed disparate investigations into the nature of collective life. With the rise of modern political theory and economics, however, writers from Machiavelli to Max Weber placed the machinations of power at center stage while deeming matters of caretaking impracticable, unsophisticated, or naïve.

The writings of Erasmus are emblematic of the latter tendency. His *Complaint of Peace* personifies and deliberately feminizes Thomist ethics, which insisted upon the theological significance of the political and subordinated questions of statecraft and commerce to the mystery of divine grace. In Erasmus's hands, the Thomist position becomes an unworldly goddess, "Peace," whose lofty incredulity at the brutality of men's affairs is characterized as ethically noble but politically unrealistic and philosophically guileless. Subsequently, modern thought imagined the state as providing only the most threadbare care in the form of minimal rights and protections, while relocating care's key quandaries to the extragovernmental domains of civil society, aesthetics, and the domestic sphere. At the same time, modernity increasingly discovered power everywhere, from repressive state apparatuses to unconscious sexual fantasies. This process corresponds to what has been called the "immanentization" of the political in modernity. The term generally describes the early modern shift of politics away from its former basis in scholastic theology toward a new sober grounding in material actuality. Here, however, I wish to be more precise about the metaphysical transformation it entails. The immanentization of the political gradually replaced the distant centered action and boundless metaphysics that organized late medieval political theology with the decentered, contiguous, and bounded haecceity of modern political philosophy. Power became the basis of this all-pervasive haecceity, while care was consigned to the role of a weak feminine supplement.

Consequently, the dominant tendencies in critical theory have been to treat care as a deceptive tool of state and capitalist domination; a social response to careless political and economic institutions; or an oppositional mode of social empowerment, be it civic, aesthetic, or domestic. Michel Foucault pursued each approach more or less separately. He critiqued pastoral care as a mode of political power; noted both the immanent creativity of "biopolitics" and the "biopower" of state racism; and revived the Socratic "care of self" as an ulterior practice of worldly ethics.[1] Adorno, by contrast, interwove the three approaches. Through his practice of negative illumination, he complicated Marxist dismissals of the bourgeois family and its affections and drew an inverted image of hope from the systemic failure of familial love under heedless monopoly capitalism. "Unpolitical attempts to break out of the bourgeois family usually only lead to deeper entanglement in such, and sometimes it seems as if the disastrous germ-cell of society, the family, is simultaneously the nourishing germ-cell of the uncompromising will for a different one."[2] Uncovering the unconscious political promise of bourgeois affection, yet unable to detect a "nourishing germ-cell" within the money relation itself, critical theorists such as Adorno pose the problem of care in terms of state and capitalist repression, social answers to a careless political economy, and the utopian potential of various counter-practices.

Though a persistent theme in the history of critical theory, care has never been linked to its dominant instrument: namely, the boundless money relation upon which the modern totality depends. Instead, the immanentization of the political rendered money's limitless public center illegible. Indeed, to attain the status of a private and alienable thisness, the Liberal money form *had* to exorcize care's anxious infinitude from the center of political and economic life. It needed to make power's circumscribed thisness the chief object of political thought. In a sense, Liberal money is the very process by which modernity simultaneously immanentized power and contracted care's horizon around a similarly decentered and immanent haecceity. Moreover, because critical theory has hitherto neglected to thematize—let alone critically engage—this process, its own efforts at thinking care have been radically curtailed. These constrictions are felt throughout the history of critical theory, but they become most evident in the political hopelessness that permeates critical theory's treatment of the aesthetic in the neoliberal period.

As I noted in the previous chapter, early and mid-twentieth century critical theorists largely took for granted the historical gravitas of the aesthetic, which they variously opposed to the money relation. Even as they debated the project's social role, efficacy, and import, critical theorists of this period shared a fundamental belief in the aesthetic's capacities for counteracting money's apparent carelessness, be it in the form of artworks, quotidian practices, or critical theory's own methodological commitments to thinking the totality in terms of sensuousness, particularity, and the non-identical. As midcentury American Keynesianism yielded to a global neoliberalism, and modernism to postmodern and contemporary aesthetics, critical theory enlarged and differentiated such commitments, encompassing matters of gender, race, sexuality, and ecology. But as capital rolled back labor's midcentury gains and tax repeals made the state appear ever more broke, critical theorists increasingly lost faith in the aesthetic's grand historical promise. Paralyzed by historical circumstances and bereft of means for conceiving money as a boundless center of caretaking, critical theory has since pursued the bleak task of carving out modest corners of hope within an otherwise hopeless structure of power.

Modern Monetary Theory points critical theory beyond these philosophical and affective strictures. Revealing how money comprises a boundless public center, MMT permits critical theorists to think of the monetary relation as the crux of caretaking and thereby invert the immanentization of politics enacted by Liberal money. The result enables critical theory to release money's untapped capacities and transcend the aesthetic project's neoliberal exhaustion. It saves contemporary aesthetics by dissolving the historical dialectic between money and the aesthetic and situates the latter wholly within the former's care. I call this the *proto-aesthetic* dimension of the monetary relation that can be revealed only by conceptual and affective labor. Critical theory must, therefore, loosen its historical attachments to power's shifting vicissitudes and risk the embarrassments of care's apparent guilelessness. Without this affective labor, its conceptual tools remain inert. It is not enough to merely think and imagine care as the center of modern life; one instead must dare to assume the insufferable position of Erasmus's scorned goddess.

Whither the Center?

Money is the center of caretaking in modernity. Yet several real world examples seem to undermine MMT's grounding of money in centralized governance and, with this, my thesis that money constitutes a center of care. For example, one may point to constricting international metal standards; governments that legally adopt the state currency of foreign hegemons; colonial currencies that force money systems upon people for purposes of exploitation; currency pegs that fix the value of currencies in postcolonial states to neoimperialist regimes; or the calamitous euro project, which has turned former command posts of world imperialism into the debtor colonies of multinational financial institutions. All these monetary arrangements restrict government spending to what can be taxed and borrowed from the private sector. Each implies a radical noncoincidence between the nation-state's geographical boundaries and global financial relations. Moreover, every one of the foregoing examples subjects politically sovereign states to the whims of foreign governments, international financial markets, and multinational corporations. Thus one might reasonably conclude that MMT's account of the money relation applies solely to states that issue their own currencies and that can therefore authorize spending *ad infinitum*. If money can be said to constitute a boundless center of caretaking, then it does so only within states that are monetarily, and not merely politically, sovereign. Moreover, because only a dozen or so states currently meet this criterion, an empirically or institutionally based argument that money comprises the center of modern caretaking appears overstated if not fallacious.

When it comes to money, however, things are almost never as they seem. According to MMT, centralized governments organize, support, and enforce fiscal restrictions. They also set the floor for all actions of global corporations and financial institutions. If money appears to constitute a global, unruly, and essentially fractured relation, then this imaginary owes primarily to political entanglements in and between centralized governments that together envision the money relation as a private alienable this-ness. Money thus remains a boundless public center, but that center is splintered, obscured, and repressed. The money relation might therefore be said to compose a structural, or transcendental, locus that is always grounded in centralized governance. Such a locus shapes complex geopolitical entanglements. It gives rise to multifaceted global interactions that outstrip state boundaries, restrict fiscal spending, and foster multiple forms of injustice around the world. Through all this, however, money retains its transcendental locus in centralized governance. It cannot be reduced to the facticity of global commercial transactions.

So construed, money sits at the center of power, yet its capacity for care still comes up against the immanentization of the political domain. As I have suggested, modern political discourse charges governance with only meager responsibility for political subjects, places the ultimate source of care outside the government, and poses the problem of politics primarily in terms of power. Thus, however diversely, Thomas Hobbes, John Locke, and Jean-Jacques Rousseau begin their accounts in a "state of nature" comprising power relations between immediate social actors, be they essentially antagonistic (Hobbes), neutral (Locke), or almost nonexistent (Rousseau). These direct power relations become the basis for the rise of modern money through barter. And the political domain emerges when such associations are aggregated, scaled up, and finally subordinated to a formal authority.

Understood as such, governance marks an appendage to the play of social forces. It concentrates social power among disparate and often opposing groups. It steadies social antagonisms from the sidelines. And in eschewing absolutist arguments for sovereignty's divine foundations, Hobbes, Locke, and Rousseau reduce the state to nothing but an expression or representation of a society's immanent powers. Meanwhile, matters of care become an exchange or trade-off. One chooses to give up the absolute freedom of association known to an unprotected state of nature in order to gain certain minimal rights and protections. At the same time, the assistance afforded by government remains not only paltry and supplemental but also constrained by power's immanent and finite expressions as well as by tax revenues and bond sales.

With his critique of so-called primitive accumulation, Marx presents a counter–origin story for modern political economy that would seem to put pressure on the Enlightenment myths of origination.[3] Yet Marx's now widely cited primitive accumulation narrative only strengthens the immanentization of the political and modernity's reduction of politics to power. This story is marked by the specter of the tribal or aboriginal. But as a historical materialist, Marx sets his primitive accumulation scenario in early modern Europe, rejecting Enlightenment reveries about long lost pasts. Repudiating the Enlightenment's freely chosen political contract as a bourgeois scam, Marx sees money's appearance in early modernity as a case of unilateral political domination involving the bare expropriation of labor and resources by landlords. According to Marx's account, monetary systems surfaced when ruling classes elected to subordinate and essentially rob populations, which were at the time distinct and self-subsistent. By privatizing lands previously designated as commons, property-owning classes divorced non-owning classes from the means of production and forced them to labor in exchange for meager wages. From this perspective, then, bourgeois contract theory transmutes into a devious power play in which elite minorities confiscate the means and fruits of social labor from communities with whom they do not already associate and produce. With this, however, Marx's primitive accumulation story puts into sharp relief the most bankrupt assumption behind modernity's immanentization of politics and economics: the notion that modern political economy arises out of an originary *non-rapport*, that money forges a relation between organically dissociated groups, and that this coming together necessarily involves forced subservience and material theft.

Somewhat surprisingly, MMT economists themselves offer no serious challenge to the Enlightenment conception of politics. Despite its radical intervention into contemporary political economy, MMT proffers several origin stories. But these generally presuppose the haecceity of organic relations and think of political governance according to Weber's definition as a monopoly on the legitimate use of physical force.[4] The most frequently cited scenario puts a chartalist twist on the Marxist primitive accumulation theory. This story is typically presented as an imaginative construct designed to lay bare money's underlying operations and is often expressly divorced from any specific historical context. Initially, government levies a direct tax on a population along with a threat of punishment for failure to pay. Whether physical, material, or corporeal, this threat generates the condition of unemployment by forcing persons to earn government notes via wage labor or private profit.[5] In this sense MMT economists contend that money is backed more by state violence than by precious commodities such as gold. Furthermore, when MMTers discuss the erection of ancient monetary systems such as those in Sumer, Babylon, and Egypt, they narrate transition from a nonmonetary to a monetary society as passing from a world of organic egalitarian associations to one based in economic inequality and social hierarchy.[6] Much like Marxist primitive accumulation theory, then, MMT's primary origin scenario reduces political economy to power and presumes an initial nonrelation between money's users.

MMT also offers a second and comparatively less violent scenario. This story positions money as a redistribution mechanism grounded in pre-monetary systems of retribution and punishment. Based on the historical research of chartalist Alfred Mitchell Innes on the Anglo-Saxon and Germanic "wergild" tradition, this story depicts the emergence of modern money as a governmental means for settling feuds. In this tradition, local authorities punished criminals by collecting taxes in kind and then offering the appropriated goods as recompense to wronged families. Eventually, governments came to convert this redistribution mechanism into a monetary system in which fines and payments were charged in an abstract unit of account.

In time, these governmental money systems outstripped their original purpose as instruments of legal punishment and feud settlement. They began to mobilize social production for private purposes and for the provisioning of labor and resources for public purposes. Thus, while MMT's second origin scenario retains the widely shared assumption that modern money arises from a system of violence and punishment, it pushes against the modern immanentization of politics and reduction of political economy to power by suggesting that monetary communities involve already associated peoples and that the money relation may mean more than merely inequality and coercion. The trouble is that MMT neither explicitly thematizes these complications nor overtly challenges modern thought's reduction of political economy to power.

A notable exception within the world of neochartalism, however, is the work of contemporary historian Christine Desan. In her book *Making Money: Coin, Currency, and the Making of Capitalism*, Desan conceives money's origins in a manner that circumvents the immanentization of the political. In so doing, she indicates what it might mean to imagine the money relation as the center of care in the modern world. Desan painstakingly tracks the historical rise of chartal money in early modern England, offering a detailed critique of its seventeenth-century privatization and imagined decentralization in the context of a legal system influenced by Liberal philosophy. Desan devotes several pages to theorizing money's original constitution, wherein she abstracts from her empirical research into English law:

> Money appears in groups that draw upon the contributions of members to support themselves or their activities. It arises when a stakeholder, acting for the group, uses its singular position to specify and entail value in a way that no individual

or bargaining pair of individuals can do. The stakeholder gives a marker to people who contribute resources earlier to the group than they are due and takes the marker back, like a receipt, from those people at the time of reckoning. In an illiquid world—one bereft of a common measure—the marker used to assess the resources will have an extraordinary status: it creates a standard for goods and services that could not previously be compared in a unit shared by everyone. One more twist makes the measure money. If the stakeholder takes back the units from anyone's hand, those units will convey material value that is useful to anyone who owes a contribution to the center. The result is a token that fixes or entails value in a way that both the stakeholder and individuals can use, a novel accomplishment in a world without an agreed-upon way to measure and transfer resources.[7]

Several features stand out in Desan's story that will be familiar to any student of chartalist political economy. Instead of treating money as private token-cum-contract that emerges from the primordial soup of barter, she argues that money is created when a representative stakeholder establishes a common mark and measure, which facilitates material contributions to the community center. Money is also a temporal project, according to Desan. It requires the ongoing receipt or reckoning of community tokens by the center, a continuous temporal labor of redemption.

Most unique to Desan's account, however, is the implicit political ontology that subtends its conception of the money relation. Departing from modernity's immanent politics, Desan's story of money's origins does not posit a power struggle between distinct groups to explain how one group comes to subordinate another. Instead, she assumes that money comes into being within a political community that has been long associated.

However subtly, Desan also emphasizes that social dependency precedes the institution of money and becomes reorganized through the formation of a monetary economy. Arguing that the central stakeholder "uses its singular position to specify and entail value in a way that no individual or bargaining pair of individuals can do," Desan stresses the reliance of individuals and their immediate associations upon the governing center before, during, and after the transition to a money economy.[8] Describing the principal aim of such a system as "draw[ing] upon the contributions of members to support themselves or their activities," her theorization situates social dependency and collective support within the money relation.[9] She places the question of care at the heart of the political.

Consequently, Desan's story of money's origins courts suspicion and potential embarrassment à la Erasmus's feminized naïf. Indeed, we might suspect that her underdeveloped gesture trucks in class-blind egalitarianism or class-conditioned fantasies of social harmony. We might therefore resist her account by turning to the agonistic theory of money proffered by chartalist sociologist Geoffrey Ingham. Drawing on Weber's writings, Ingham treats political economy as a contest for power, contending that "money is a weapon in the struggle for . . . existence."[10] However, I think it important to suspend such judgments since they reinscribe modernity's reduction of politics to power and close off the riddle of care that Desan's theory of money opens up. Rather than retreat from this threshold, let us pursue means for expanding it.

The Unheard-of Center

To advance Desan's suggestion that money is the center of collective support, I turn to an alternative and historically older genealogy of care that courses through modern thought. Care, according to this conception, composes the *mystery of collective interdependence* and the *riddling locus toward which every member of a society variably leans.* In this view, care describes neither positive affections nor deliberate acts of assistance that may be said to realize, supplement, or oppose an immanent field of power. Instead, care is an enigmatic and fundamentally open social charge. It derives from the structure of our dependence, rending and incurring the social field around the mysterious center upon which everyone depends. I argue that *care's center ontologically precedes the money relation*, but money becomes the dominant means for politically organizing the riddle of social dependence during the modern period. The way properly to contest and enlarge money's boundless public capacity is to politicize the monetary relation from the vantage of care. Doing so permits an unabashed affirmation of Desan's theory of money as social dependency, avoiding modernity's patriarchal reduction of politics to power as well as conflict-obscuring fantasies of social harmony that critics misogynistically dismiss as feminine naïveté.

The alternative genealogy of care upon which I draw is traceable to the so-called myth of care, or "Cura," attributed to the first-century Roman poet Gaius Julius Hyginus. Hyginus's parable is brief, so I will quote it in full:

Once when "Care" was crossing a river, she saw some clay; she thoughtfully took up a piece and began to shape it. While she was meditating on what she had made, Jupiter came by. "Care" asked him to give it spirit, and this he gladly granted. But when she wanted her name to be bestowed upon it, he forbade this, and demanded that it be given his name instead. While "Care" and Jupiter were disputing, Earth arose and desired that her own name be conferred on the creature, since she had furnished it with part of her body. They asked Saturn to be their arbiter, and he made the following decision, which seemed a just one: "Since you, Jupiter, have given its spirit, you shall receive that spirit at its death; and since you, Earth, have given its body, you shall receive its body. But since 'Care' first shaped this creature, she shall possess it as long as it lives. And because there is now a dispute among you as to its name, let it be called *homo*, for it is made out of *humus* (earth). "[11]

Historically, Hyginus's parable has been interpreted as a gynephilic counter-myth to the patriarchal origin stories that dominate Western tradition. Such readings note the parable's affirmation of Cura's feminine perspective as opposed to that of the masculine gods. Her irresolvable predicaments, moreover, are central to the myth's conception of the human. "The lifelong care of the human that would be undertaken by Cura entails both an earthly, bodily element that is pulled down to the ground (worry) and a spirit-element that strives upward to the divine," writes theologian Warren T. Reich. "The positive side of care dominates in this story, for the primordial role of Care is to hold the human together in wholeness while cherishing it."[12] Caught in the stream of life, Cura is pitched between worldly burdens and spiritual uplift as she strives to shape the living figure that becomes her charge.

Still, there remains a less remarked upon, yet no less significant, dimension of the Cura fable. It pertains to the myth's treatment of care's signification and locatability. For feminist philosophers such as Jean Graybeal and Katrin Froesse, Hyginus's story may avow the importance of Cura's feminine struggle, but it also dramatizes the patriarchal repression of Care's name and locus.[13] Father Saturn's apparently just arbitration allows Cura to bear the human being throughout its life, but when it comes time to designate and locate this creation, he names it *homo* after *humus*, meaning mere ground or dirt. This designation reduces homo's activity to Earth's material thisness and renders Cura's thoughtful mediation of matter and meaning, earth and heaven, to something Fredric Jameson might call a "vanishing mediator."[14] Of course, for Jameson, this term marks a medium's sublation of antagonistic terms that will fall away when no longer needed. In this case, however, Care remains tasked with holding everything together while lacking a proper designation or a place to call her own. Homo may incidentally note Earth's role in supporting its spiritual quests for meaning. Yet as Hyginus's fable indicates, the creature will have little to no awareness of the medium responsible for these strivings and the gatherings of matter and meaning upon which they depend.

For this reason, perhaps, care persists as a minor, though significant, thread in the history of Western thought. From Socrates and Seneca to Johann Wolfgang von Goethe and Søren Kierkegaard, care qua problem, or mystery, is taken up, thought afresh, and given heterogeneous meanings. In chapter 3 I consider the historical contraction and decentering of care as part of a broader discussion of the transformation mediation undergoes in late medieval and early modern thought. For now, however, I want to focus on Martin Heidegger's early twentieth-century effort to develop an expansive notion of care as a ground for phenomenology and, later, what he designates as a "center" that has gone "unheard."[15]

In *Being and Time* Heidegger makes care the focus of his inquiry into phenomenology and what he calls "fundamental ontology."[16] The Heidegger of *Being and Time* is primarily interested in what it means to "be-in-the-world." He sets out to think the disclosure of "Being" not as a series of discrete persons, entities, and ideas but rather as singular uncoverings of an integrated environmental whole. The starting point for this investigation is the human being, who, according to Heidegger, is the only being for whom the question of "Being" is perpetually at issue. Rather than conceive this human opening through an autonomous rational agent, however, Heidegger maintains that every disclosure of Being emerges from a dependent and receptive *Dasein*, meaning "there-being," or more plainly, "being there." Dasein is always immersed in a world it has not chosen. It is "thrown" into a great social, technical, and material milieu. On account of this "thrownness," Heidegger laments, Dasein tends to fall into a narrow existence of what is immediately knowable and present-at-hand. Still, Dasein's futurity remains underdetermined and open because its thrownness charged it with an inescapable anxiety about the meaning of Being, which Heidegger calls *Sorge*, or "care."

According to *Being and Time*, care is the basis of Dasein and the source of Being's temporalization. In this conception, care means neither worrying about extant things nor actively tending to some person, tool, or situation. Instead, care is an indelible angst about the whole of Being into which Dasein has been thrown. Such is the peril of care as well as its promise. Dasein leads a narrow and detached existence, fretting over what is immediately known, named, and mastered. Yet when it projects itself upon the unknown whole that supports its impassioned everydayness, Dasein turns thrown pasts toward future ventures and discloses Being anew. Essential for this process is care's transpersonal and quasi-divine topology. Though Heidegger often approaches care as a finite and singular comportment within the world, he also shows that care is not an emanation of individuated Dasein. Rather, it arises from Being's mysterious whole in the form of an indefinite charge or "call." This call constitutes Dasein's existential debt, or "guilt," vis-à-vis the whole. Thus, far from proceeding from individuated Dasein, care expresses an omnipresent indebtedness. The anxiety that accompanies this burden becomes, meanwhile, the basis for Dasein's singularizing projects.

During the 1930s Heidegger turned toward matters of language, poiesis, and forms of ontological dwelling, moving still further away from the Enlightenment subjectivism and metaphysical hierarchies that linger in *Being and Time*. In an essay titled "What Are Poets For?" he develops the significance of care for this project through a reading of one of Rainer Maria Rilke's late poems, "Force of Gravity." Appealing to Rilke's poetic language, Heidegger characterizes care as a distinctly nonphysical force of gravity, an "including attraction" that draws together and embraces all beings.[17] Citing Rilke, Heidegger names the locus of this attractive force "the unheard-of center."[18] Decentered from merely human Dasein and unknown to modern rationality and industry, this unheard-of center holds all Being in balance and, when willingly ventured, pulls every being into the security, or care, of an open and boundless "draft":[19]

That draft is the unheard-of center of all attraction which draws all things into the boundless, and draws them for the center. This center is "there," where the gravity of the pure forces rules. To be secure is to repose safely within the drawing of the whole draft.[20]

In Heidegger's judgment, this securing center may appear insecure, even care*less*, from the objectifying perspective of modern science and industry. Yet to be truly safe and care*free*, Heidegger surmises, one must risk abandoning modernity's narrow field of concern and activity and venture without reserve into what he elsewhere calls an "all sheltering breadth."[21]

Thus, despite Heidegger's abstract and, for many, cloyingly philosophical language—not to mention his purported anti-Semitism—the philosopher's phenomenology marks a critical turning point in the modern genealogy of care. Heidegger's conception of care brings us a step closer, in fact, to money as the center of care in modernity. Making care the focus of his fundamental ontology, Heidegger does not treat it as an objectified concern or an activity that opposes creative disclosure. Instead, he presents care as an ontologically unsurpassable structure of dependence and an unavoidable omnipresent charge. Moreover, in designating its boundless horizon as an unheard-of center, Heidegger encourages us to envision care as an all-inclusive center of attraction that may have become imperceptible under patriarchal modernity but that nevertheless continues to organize being-in-the-world.

There are substantial limitations to Heidegger's philosophy of care. For one, he opposes care to political economy, despite efforts to inscribe it otherwise in modernity's complex technical and economic organization. Moreover, though Heidegger notes how "vibrations of money . . . [might] develop for themselves a kind of spirituality" in the premodern age of "beautiful" gold coinage, he nonetheless appeals to Marxist tropes of disintegration when it comes to modern monetary systems.[22] Such abstract systems, he writes, "dissolve the thingness of things . . . into the calculated market."[23] The unheard-of center permits concerted movements of weighing and assaying—a balancing at once risked and safely upheld. The contemporary merchant who "weighs and measures constantly . . . does not know the real weight of things," however. "Nor does he ever know what in himself is truly weighty and preponderant."[24]

This limitation in Heidegger's philosophy reveals a second and greater obstacle to his conception of care. Adhering to the Liberal conception of money as decentered and immanent thisness, Heidegger's construction of care presents a boundless, yet distinctly decentered center that mimics the modern metaphysics of haecceity. It thus unwittingly endorses the systematic carelessness of political economy that Heidegger seeks to answer. Though mostly repressed in his oeuvre, this connection between Liberal money's metaphysics and the metaphysics of care rears its head when Heidegger expressly meditates on the ontological properties of gold. "The splendor of gold," he writes,

> keeps and holds everything present in the unconcealedness of its appearing. . . . It entrusts world to the things and simultaneously keeps the things in the splendor of world. The world grants to things their presence. Things bear world. World grants things.[25]

Here Heidegger explicitly links the contracted trust-relation of Liberal money's metaphysics to Being's expansive bearing and granting of things in the world. His intervention takes us closer to care, but Heidegger's uncritical commitment to Being's decentered thisness disables the money relation as its boundless public center.

Declarations of Dependence

A critical model for disclosing money as the center of care does not yet exist in the modern imagination. That said, philosopher and queer theorist Judith Butler carries us to the edge of this limited imaginary by extending the Heideggerian articulation of care to the problem of political economy. Under the influence of Emmanuel Levinas and Hannah Arendt, Butler does for political economy what Heidegger did for metaphysics: she makes the quandary of our unsurpassable social dependence the basis for political critique and contestation. In so doing, Butler departs from feminist ethicists and political theorists who emphasize moral praxis. Rather than set embodied caretaking against abstract political power, she answers neoliberalism's systemic carelessness by politicizing the constitutive dependencies that implicate all subjects from the most to the least empowered.

To be sure, notions of social dependence have informed Butler's thought since her early work on French-Hegelian philosophies of desire and gender performativity.[26] Yet dependency's intractable horizon comes to the fore in her later turn to ethico-political philosophy. An especially sharp demonstration of this thinking comes in "On Cruelty," a critical review of Jacques Derrida's book *The Death Penalty: Vol. 1*. Derrida's text, which calls for the end of the death penalty, warns against the hegemonic morality that undergirds most pleas for abolition. This moral logic, he argues, substitutes prolonged sadistic punishment for untimely death. It also places the abolitionist's aggression under the cover of an ethically unimplicated neighborly love. In this sense Derrida follows Friedrich Nietzsche's well-known argument in *On the Genealogy of Morals* about the relationship between violence, morality, and law.[27] In Nietzsche's account Judeo-Christian morality develops out of an amoral creditor-debtor contract meant to exact retribution for injurious acts of violence. For Nietzsche as much as Derrida, an aggressive will to power always precedes this contract. "At issue," writes Derrida, "is a diagnosis of a cruelty that has no contrary because it is originary."[28] The exchange contract mediates primordial aggression through a principle of equivalence it establishes "between the crime and the punishment, between the injury and the price to be paid."[29] The trouble begins, however, when the Judeo-Christian tradition attempts to moralize this exchange. At once repressing and redoubling originary cruelty in the name of righteousness and beneficence, Judeo-Christians adopt a "slave morality" that renders evil the will to power and makes resentment, or *ressentiment*, of power the basis for the social contract. This inverted moralism then becomes the legal foundation for modern sovereignty and the state's authority over life and death. Thus, for Derrida, abolishing the death penalty means disavowing life's originary cruelty and, after Freud, the destructive "death drive" that pulses beneath social projects. To do otherwise, Butler affirms, may convert "the death penalty . . . into its opposite" and "unleash[] a celebratory affirmation of its destructiveness."[30]

Despite this affirmation, however, Butler breaks with Derrida. "Are there . . . reasons for wanting to keep the other alive," she wonders, "that do not primarily rely on our wish to continue torturing that other, even when it isn't someone in particular, but an anonymous other or the general population?"[31] To answer this question Butler pursues an alternative psychoanalytic conception of filiation and ambivalence, one predicated upon the subject's ineradicable dependence on otherness. In this account, "there is no overcoming ambivalence in love, since we are always at risk of destroying what we are most attached to and vulnerable to being destroyed by those on whom we are most dependent."[32] Locating this vision in Freud's writings, Butler uncovers it in passing remarks in *The Interpretation of Dreams*, after it emerges full-blown in the essay "Mourning and Melancholia." Later, ambivalence in love becomes Melanie Klein's central concern and the basis for the "object-relations" school of psychoanalysis that her work inspires. For Klein, Butler explains, "the fantasy of destroying becomes coupled with the fear of losing those on whom one is absolutely dependent."[33] Thus, in Klein's view, primary aggression arises in tandem with life-affirming affection and remains wholly within the "absolute" horizon of social dependence throughout the subject's existence.

With this account of ambivalence rooted in dependence, Butler reposes Derrida's approach to the death penalty and expands his argument to develop a more capacious foundation for politics. For Derrida, abolishing the death penalty means facing a potentially perilous will to power that always precedes and exceeds the preservation of life. Butler, by contrast, proceeds from the constitutive dilemma of subjective dependence. Circumventing self-interest and the will to power, she grounds the very legibility of the subject in the other toward which the "I" never ceases to "lean":

Since individuation is never complete, and dependency never really overcome, a broader ethical dilemma emerges. It isn't a matter of calculating that destroying them would probably be a bad idea. It is a matter of recognizing that dependency fundamentally defines us: it is something I never quite outgrow, no matter how old and how individuated I may seem. And it isn't that you and I are the same; rather, it is that we invariably lean towards each other and on each other. And it is impossible to think about either of us without the other. If I seek to preserve your life, it is not only because it is in my self-interest to do so, or because I have wagered that it will bring about better consequences for me. It is because I am already tied to you in a social bond without which this "I" cannot be thought.[34]

Because the "I" is tethered in a dependent social bond, state violence against the other threatens the background on which the self relies. From here, Butler moves from the death penalty as a specific case to the systemic precarity authorized by the neoliberal state. Linking state-authorized death to the penal system, she ties it to histories of debt peonage, unfree labor, and poverty that continue to damage collective existence. Butler then calls for critical praxis to "expose the various different mechanisms for destroying life, and to find ways, however conflicted and ambivalent, of preserving lives that would otherwise be lost."[35]

In so doing, Butler redresses Heidegger as much as Derrida, returning care to the polis beyond which he situates the unheard-of center. Indeed, if Heidegger wagers well-being beyond political economy, then Butler makes economics and politics the sites for risking his non-substantialist topology of care. A poststructuralist, she may avoid Heidegger's use of the term *center*, yet Butler persistently links social dependency to centralized governance. In this view, the center marks neither an aggregate of empirical institutions nor the field of transcendental conditions these institutions establish. Rather, for Butler, the center composes a site toward which members of a society necessarily lean. It is, in fact, nothing other than dependency's inward leanings. For this reason, the center knows no substantial foundation or locus; it precedes material structures and exceeds their conditions of possibility. It is, in short, the very structure of care itself, a figure of collective interdependence that joins centrifugal associations and contests in an inescapable, centripetal vortex.

Conceived as such, care does not contest political power so much as political power's structuration by economics and politics. In writings from *Frames of War* to *Notes Toward a Performative Theory of Assembly*, Butler formulates a theory of embodied political contestation that complicates modernity's reduction of politics to power and the one-sided pleas for emancipation, empowerment, and freedom it motivated. These pleas, though crucial for resisting enslavement, imprisonment, and other forms of political control, risk obscuring dilemmas of collective dependence. They render inarticulable demands for life's enduring infrastructural support. To be sure, Butler recognizes the inextricability of power and care, but she also distinguishes the problem of subjugation from the riddles of dependence:

> On the one hand, everyone is dependent on social relations and enduring infrastructures in order to maintain a livable life, so there is no getting rid of that dependency. On the other hand, that dependency, though not the same as a condition of subjugation, can easily become one. The dependency of human creatures on sustaining and supporting infrastructural life shows that the organization of infrastructure is intimately tied with an enduring sense of individual life: how life is endured, and with what degree of suffering, livability, or hope.[36]

Social dependency can and often does devolve into subjugation. However, Butler contends, dependency remains an inescapable dilemma and social obligation. Irreducible to political oppression, this dilemma outstrips the language of power. It organizes the political and economic infrastructures that sustain social existence, condition individuated action, and shape struggles for power.

For this reason Butler calls for modes of embodied assembly and collective performance that expressly politicize social dependence against neoliberal carelessness. Hardly new, these assemblies include the likes of Occupy Wall Street, the Arab Spring, anti-austerity protests in Europe, and ongoing Black Lives Matter demonstrations in American cities. In such gatherings, those who are systemically imperiled and uncared for converge in spontaneous and sensational democratic assemblages. Rendering social dependencies corporeal and perceptible, they "not only . . . bring the material urgencies of the body . . . but [also]," writes Butler, "make those needs central to the demands of politics."[37] In this way heterogeneous ensembles enact their "right to appear" both in and as public. They also make the center upon which the public relies demonstrably accountable.

Such assemblies may, at times, look like assertions of autonomy from and against a subjugating center. What Butler shows, however, is the extent to which these demonstrations affirm social dependence and render the mystery of collective caretaking public and palpable. Every performative assembly "asserts and instates the body in the midst of the political field, and . . . in its expressive and signifying function, delivers a bodily demand for a more livable set of economic, social, and political conditions no longer afflicted by induced forms of precarity."[38] Such actions wage struggles over public space that bear witness to social suffering. They push an invisible infrastructural background into a politicized public foreground. Finally, they make embodied collective demands for public support adequate to sustaining and developing collective existence. "Human action depends upon all sorts of supports," writes Butler:

> it is always supported action. But in the case of public assemblies, we see quite clearly not only that there is a struggle over what will be public space, but a struggle as well over those basic ways in which we are, as bodies, supported in the world—a struggle against disenfranchisement, effacement, and abandonment.[39]

Public assemblies do not merely fight for increased power over the public sphere. They politicize the background institutions that support the play of power. More important, they do so by universalizing dilemmas of social dependence as the field from which every "I" must henceforth be thought.

Of course, Butler neither invents the politics of care nor is the first to theorize them. Political demands for caretaking date to fifteenth-century protests against rising bread prices and remain central to historically persistent assertions of the right to justly remunerated work. In the twentieth century the problem of care becomes increasingly self-conscious, marking struggles for race, gender, and sexual justice and the politicization of welfare and un- and underpaid labor. Meanwhile, care's place in politics can be found in the writings and speeches of civil rights leaders Bayard Rustin, Dr. Martin Luther King Jr., and Coretta Scott King; in works by feminist theorists from Carol Hanisch to Nancy Fraser; and in the field of feminist ethics inaugurated by Carol Gilligan's *In a Different Voice*. In each work, care transcends merely private or civic phenomena to become a politically organized activity that mobilizes social cohesion against a destructive will to power.

What makes Butler's contribution genuinely novel is the way

care structures politics from the start and, in so doing, reconfigures the political as such. Like other theorists, Butler situates care as political contestation, yet unlike them, she does not subordinate care to power. Care neither expresses domination nor serves as an external supplement or oppositional force. In this way Butler refuses to naturalize the modern immanentization of politics and instead reimagines the political domain, grounding it where struggles for power meet shared quandaries of interdependence. One might encapsulate her insights as follows: *care is inextricable from but irreducible to power, and the political is the site of this very entanglement.* Indeed, Butler installs the problem of dependency in the political sphere's center. Politicizing Heidegger's care, she conceives an all-encompassing dilemma that exempts no social actor. Power is not, therefore, easily wrenched from the political domain. Instead, struggles for power confront the riddle of social dependence and care's disquieting charge.

With this, Butler enlarges the social ontology that undergirds care politics. She sharpens the sense of what it means to foreground the background infrastructures that support demonstrative publics. Concurrently, Butler's politicization of Heideggerian care suggests wholly new premises for the practice of critical theory, particularly when set inside a critique of modernity's immanentization of politics. Such is my contention based on the work of Heidegger and Butler. To join care to dependence and place both at the center of political economy is to point beyond modernity's reduction of politics to power and open critical theory to new possibilities for imagining reliable and nourishing public infrastructures. Butler brings us close, I have suggested, to thinking money as the center of care in modernity. Tethering care to constitutive dependence and dependency to an expansive infrastructural imagination, she not only locates the problem of political economy in centralized governance but also loosens the contracted metaphysics of thisness presumed by Nietzsche, Heidegger, and Derrida.

Still, an unreconciled contradiction prevents Butler from thinking money as the center of care. Though she conceives political economy *in general* as a center toward which dependent subjects lean, Butler tacitly accepts the Liberal ontology of money and its zero-sum contract. The result relinquishes money to the story of debt and retribution that underwrites Nietzsche's will to power and Derrida's primary cruelty. It also compels Butler to condemn money qua center and situate constitutive dependence and care beyond the supposed violence of the money relation. "We have . . . to ask," she writes in response to Derrida's critique of the death penalty, "whether there are social relations outside the terms of debt and payment, relations that might be understood as being outside capital, or outside the psychic and moral terms by which injury-cum-debt authorizes incarceration and the death penalty."[40] To reconfigure the preservation of life as Derrida formulates it, Butler thinks she must move *outside* the monetary economy with its originary cruelty, zero-sum struggle for power, and sadistic Judeo-Christian morality. She sacrifices the instrument that presumably mediates care politics. What we discover in Butler's project, then, is a desire to treat political economy as the center of care, even as her commitment to Liberal money neither accommodates nor supports its tremendous demands. She thus disregards Hyginus's warning in the fable of Cura and represses care's name and locus within the domain she wishes to elevate.

To fulfill Butler's wish for critical theory necessitates both recuperating and unabashedly naming care's vanishing mediator, which knows no other locus or designation in modernity than the money form itself. Money is truly the center of care in modernity. And as MMT helps us see, this center holds the capacity to cultivate the totality outside the Liberal money form's zero-sum morality and the politics of resentment. Thus, while historically critical theory came into existence in order to critique and eventually negate money's abstract value, critique after MMT must radically affirm money's boundless public center and politicize its limitless capacities for care. Meanwhile, what is needed to bring answerability to neoliberal misery are neither combative assertions of autonomy nor the plaintive chants of peace. Instead, we require what, in the spirit Butler's intervention, I call *declarations of dependence*: impassioned demonstrations of thrown social belonging that involve everyone in care's riddling obligations.

The Proto-Aesthetic

Caught in a shifting and unpredictable world, Hyginus's Cura is charged with lending shape and support to a sentient figure made of wet, sensuous matter. If care is essentially an embodied and sensual problem, then thinking money as the center of care in modernity demands accounting for how an abstract public instrument comes variously to cultivate and impoverish sensuous being-in-the-world. However, since modern critical inquiries into sensuous experience have historically opposed monetary abstraction to embodied sensuality, such an account must transcend the category of the aesthetic as formerly conceived and rearticulate this relation along more fertile lines. For this reason, we need to turn now to the proto-aesthetic dimension of the modern monetary relation. A compound construction, it combines the originary meaning of the Greek term *aesthesis*—that is, sensuous feeling—with the prefix *proto*, which designates an existence *prior to* the aesthetic's modern designation as an automatous domain.

To begin understanding monetary abstraction as a proto-aesthetic relation means insisting that money's boundless public center shapes and upholds sensuous life, even when it does so in a poor or unjust manner. Money may enrich or impoverish material experience. It may expand and contract sensory horizons. As a proto-aesthetic apparatus, however, money is never subject to the drama of gain and loss that defines the Liberal money form's fantasmatic alienability. Indeed, so long as a currency-issuing government taxes its citizens and compels them to work, finances public infrastructures, and maintains welfare services, the police, and penal institutions, money remains a constant proto-aesthetic force that cannot be dispossessed. For this reason, money's proto-aesthetic dimension must be distinguished from modern aesthetic praxis. In modern aesthetics the prospect of sensory expansion is something added to and typically distinguished from everyday commerce. As a consequence the aesthetic involves a similar metaphysical play of presence and absence to what one finds in the Liberal monetary metaphysics. By contrast, money's proto-aesthetic may be likened to Cura's enduring and anxious attention. Whether supporting financial speculation or food stamps, bridge repair, or incarceration, money is never unburdened from engendering and maintaining the conditions of sensory existence.

The proto-aesthetic dimension of money must be understood, furthermore, to unfold holistically: it proceeds from and returns to the particular from the general. In this sense it differs from the mathematical specificity that orients price determination in modern economics. It also departs from the qualitative particularity that animates modern aesthetics. Instead, money's proto-aesthetic operates at a macrological scale, creating the sensuous conditions for social life in general. In practice, this means both the quantity and quality, the spacing and timing, of government's monetary output shape the material circumstances within which sensory experiences take place. To understand this macrology, one might consider what happens to embodied existence when governments do not spend enough and in the right places: unemployment expands. Bargaining power diminishes. Wages are suppressed, and working conditions degrade. Discriminatory hiring intensifies. Resentment surges. Social antagonism deepens; health worsens; and homelessness proliferates. Public spaces deteriorate. Private places fortify. Crime increases; the police are militarized and weaponized; and prisons enlarge. At the same time, purchasing power collapses, while private debt multiplies. Wealth concentrates. Capital exploits overseas markets, and supply chains generate subpar goods. As a result financiers overspeculate. Markets go bust. Production contracts; and ecological welfare hinges on feckless government regulation and green entrepreneurship. Put simply, the social totality trembles and lurches, while individuals, families, and firms leverage everything they have to stay afloat. Sensuous associations differentiate themselves against a total background. This is the nature of money's proto-aesthetic dimension. It signifies the relationship between a boundless public center and the field of sensuous particulars that money organizes.

Modern Monetary Theory's conception of unemployment and proposed "job guarantee," or JG, provide the most direct and holistic mechanism for contesting and cultivating money's proto-aesthetic field. Consequently a JG permits us to politicize money's proto-aesthetic field directly, at once circumventing and transforming the register of the particular that has blinded Liberal modernity. For MMT, employment is a fundamentally political as opposed to economic problem. Private investors and automation do not disemploy people. Rather, public spending is responsible for the unemployment level. This means that politics condition poverty, precarity, and hostility and can, therefore, transform them. MMT's JG is precisely such a political mechanism. Ensuring everyone's right to living-wage employment and sufficient public services, it shapes the quality of sensuous life as a whole.

More specifically, the JG is federally funded and locally administered. It is a universal, voluntary, and non-discriminatory program that offers wages and healthcare to persons willing and able to participate in meaningful communal projects. In so doing, the JG merges worker experience and interest with pressing public needs. It shifts with emerging wants rather than fit employees into extant positions. The JG provides, for instance, child and elder care facilities that socialize what Marxofeminist Nancy Fraser has called the "hidden abode" of unpaid care labor. It supplies environmental cleanup, retrofitting, and beautification services as well as cultural centers and social documentation programs that help communities imagine and shape the transformations the JG makes possible.[41] Meant to operate alongside, not replace, existing welfare programs, the JG's size varies with the business cycle, expanding in times of recession and contracting with private sector growth.

Indeed, in addition to eliminating poverty and abolishing systemic abandonment and exclusion, the JG becomes a public instrument for politically contesting and shaping the broad conditions of sensuous material existence. Presently, government underspending maintains a reserve of unemployed workers, giving capital de facto reign over social production within a system of perpetual crisis. Under the JG, however, the public determines the values of social production, forcing private employers to outbid the public sector in order to stay in business. In addition to stabilizing profits and bringing security to the business cycle, the JG sets private enterprise atop a democratically constituted foundation that can be augmented, expanded, and reconfigured. The JG thus creates a "floor" for social production by establishing what MMT economists call the "labor standard of value."[42] As opposed to gold or silver standards, which purportedly lend value to money by pegging currencies to precious metal markets, the labor standard politicizes the determination of value by remunerating specific forms of social participation and discouraging destructive and unsustainable ones. In this way politics govern working conditions and hours as well as expectations and aims. Private innovation and competition cease to operate, meanwhile, at the expense of human flourishing. In fact, by decoupling the floor of the economy from the profit motive, the JG realizes diverse, even antagonistic, communal desires while pursuing a so-called degrowth strategy of energy efficiency, resource conservation, and minimal waste. It also serves as a launching pad for radical reorganizations of social production, including worker-owned cooperatives and experiments in alternative life-work arrangements.

The JG thus provides public infrastructure for contesting and cultivating money's proto-aesthetic field. It promises neither heaven on earth nor a triumphant end to history wherein antagonisms cease. Still, if fought for and won, the JG stands to function as not only an economic floor for collective production but also a *sensory floor* for worldly experience. Liberal money's threat of unemployment enervates the senses and hardens the sensorium against a hemorrhaging haecceity. The JG, however, envelops and expands the senses, providing everyone with an abiding stream of new projects, social connections, and embodied experiences. This means that rather than forcefully break up and reconstitute collective experience in the name of positive revolutionary values, the JG's sensory floor works to support and differentiate the conditions of sensuous experience in a messy and incongruous world.

Since money has not historically been recognized as the center of care in modernity, money's proto-aesthetic dimension has remained invisible to the majority of critics, artists, and activists. That said, the aesthetic practice of feminist performance artist Mierle Laderman Ukeles comes close to addressing money's proto-aesthetic dimension and can therefore serve as a creative model for intervening in this field.[43] From Friedrich Schiller, the young Marx, and William Morris to Charles Baudelaire, Dada, and the Situationist International, critics of modern political economy have sought to mitigate or overcome monetary alienation by reenvisioning economic relations in the image of the aesthetic's expansive particularity. Alternatively, Ukeles turns artistic particularity toward the repressed background of social infrastructure and environmental maintenance and aims to affect the broad sensory horizon in which particular developments emerge.

Ukeles first described her project in the 1969 *Manifesto for Maintenance Art*, her plan for an exhibition titled "CARE." In the *Manifesto*, Ukeles begins by posing what she calls a "sourball" question: "After the revolution, who's going to pick up the garbage Monday morning?"[44] Social reproduction involves "two basic systems," she goes on to explain.[45] There is the system of "development," which under modern patriarchy is foregrounded and celebrated.[46] "Pure individual creation; the new; change; progress; advance; excitement; flight or fleeing."[47] Then there is the system of care, or "maintenance," which acts as background for development, often goes unpaid, and is generally feminized.[48] "Keep the dust off the pure individual creation; preserve the new; sustain the change; protect progress; defend and prolong the advance; renew the excitement; repeat the flight."[49]

Ukeles associates the system of development with the Freudian death drive: "separation; individuality; Avant-Garde par excellence; to follow one's own path to death—do your own thing; dynamic change." The system of maintenance she links to the psychoanalytic notion of the life instinct: "unification; the eternal return; the perpetuation and MAINTENANCE of the species; survival systems and operations; equilibrium." "Maintenance is a drag," she writes, "it takes all the fucking time." Yet, rather than embracing the avant-gardist mantra "make it new!" or merely exposing the unjust gendering of care work, Ukeles proposes an emphatic embrace of "maintenance art" founded upon the unvarnished slogan: "maintain it!" What emerges is an amplified commitment to maintenance, which partakes of the flights unto death care is charged with repeating, and an experience of development made to feel the drag of the daily operations needed in order to risk it all.

Ukeles's oeuvre reads like a handbook of proto-aesthetics, a catalogue of inventive projects for politically reconfiguring care's sensuous background. There are small-scale pieces such as "WASHING/TRACKS/MAINTENANCE: OUTSIDE" (1973). In that work, Ukeles scrubbed the exterior steps to the Wadsworth Atheneum Museum of Art in Hartford, Connecticut. Resonating with what has been called "institutional critique," the piece put front and center the material infrastructures needed for the exhibition of art and the human upkeep required such that visitors ascend into the space where art is displayed. Ukeles would go on to organize far more elaborate performances, a great number of which involved public budgeting and the collaboration with public institutions such as the New York Sanitation Department. Her first large-scale project with the department was titled "TOUCH SANITATION PERFORMANCE" (1979–80). Responding to a manufactured fiscal crisis in New York City that left public services underfunded and the citizens outraged, Ukeles traveled through every borough, shook the hand of each of the city's 8,500 sanitation workers, and personally thanked them "for keeping New York City alive." In a gesture that the *New York Times* would later call "a kind of secular benediction," the project's combination of meaningful contact and infrastructural breadth politicized the city's carelessness, while striving to maintain a system of maintenance under conditions of structural duress.[50]

A Tale of Two Symptoms

I wish to conclude the present chapter by proposing a method of critical interpretation that takes the proto-aesthetic as its object and is grounded in the mystery of care. To do so, I want to pursue an alternative account of the symptom that differs from the one critical theory has predominantly presupposed. I draw this alternative symptomology from the object-relations tradition to which Butler also appeals. According to the conventional Freudian view, a symptom comprises a distorted and debilitating return of an unconscious wish, which the dominant order has deemed unacceptable and conditioned the psyche to repress. I call this the "Oedipal symptom," since it revolves around the power struggle between a desirous subject and paternal law.

My interest, however, lies in a second conception of the symptom offered by psychoanalysis that diverges from Oedipal symptomology. This understanding of the symptom derives from Freud's claims referenced earlier: that dependence structures love as an ambivalent relation and that aggression toward the other risks dissolving the subject's self-consistency. This fraught dependency becomes a foundational problematic for Klein's object-relations theory and her followers, including D. W. Winnicott, Esther Bick, and Thomas Ogden. Rather than theorizing the symptom principally through the power struggle between paternal prohibition and infantile wishes, object-relations analysts tend to think symptomology through the affective knots that result from subjective dependency and, more generally, through the problem of care. As with Oedipal symptomology, this care symptom will yield diverse diagnoses and treatments. The core insight, however, concerns the caretaker's role in binding infantile perceptions and drives in early development and enveloping subjectivity within a broader social and material domain.

When caretaking is "good enough," to use Winnicott's well-known language, perceptions and drives become integrated in relation to the enigma of the caretaking environment.[51] When care is for whatever reason inadequate or fails, however, the subject will be plagued by painful and riddling symptoms. Also, while Oedipal symptomology typically revolves around the drama of having and not having, care symptomology emphasizes what Bick names care's "containing function" and the environmental envelope, or "sensory floor" in Ogden's writings, which care creates and maintains.[52] In the care symptom, sensations of loss, incoherence, and disintegration index environmental precarity at the threshold of worldly disclosure. And symptoms of this sort function as pathological attempts at self-care and as opaque messages to the other. Finally, therapeutic interpretation necessitates tracing the failed structure of care to which these messages point, and the cure involves repairing and reconstituting what Winnicott calls the subject's "confidence in the environment."[53]

Repairing the modern money relation demands a method of critical reading that is attentive not only to symptoms of power but also to the symptomology of care. Yet care cannot be reduced to the familialism that orients the object-relations tradition. In modernity, care is a problem of money in the first and last instance. Money's boundless public center constitutes sensuous existence as a whole, engendering a broad proto-aesthetic background against which care's individuated difficulties can take shape. We require a politics of care that realizes money's expansive center in finite actualizations. We need declarations of dependence that render unjust contractions of this center answerable to political contestation. However, money's boundless center is not a transparent and easily graspable locus. In addition to suffering repressions by Liberal monetary ideology, money's center moves in centrifugal patterns and works through multiple layers of social mediation. Even if a strong political commitment to transparency were to render money's mediations maximally legible, the mystery of care—Cura's ultimate name and locus—can only yield partial disclosures and affective responses.

For these reasons, a symptomology of care is needed to discern critically or, in Jamesonian parlance, "map" the totality money organizes.[54] Such a practice means reading dissonant social formations as indices of systemic carelessness. It means transmuting symptomatic longings into actionable politics. Unlike what critical theorists have formerly imagined, modern money's symptoms do not emanate from a decentered and unanswerable thisness. Rather, they mark an unseverable umbilicus, linking money as the center of caretaking in modernity to social life as a whole. Money's symptoms emerge *from* the center's failed social support systems. They return *to* the center as unconscious pleas for social security. The more care's center is repressed or disavowed, moreover, the more carelessness seems an inevitability and the more hysterical such pleas become. Critique after MMT must trace the centripetal pulses that connect these cryptic prayers, like a psychoanalyst pursuing the elusive navel of a dream.

Within this navel looms a blueprint for happiness, prefigurative of a better world. However, for critical theory to help convert modernity's unheard wishes into actionable politics, we need to treat the ill-founded metaphysics of haecceity that subtend modern mediation in general and sketch out an image of happiness by working through this regime's constitutive symptoms. In the next chapter, then, I trace the dream of haecceity to its emergence in early modern theology and reveal the navel of this dream to be a distorted plea for care.

3

Medium Congruentissimum

*The Christian doctrine nowhere holds that God was so joined
to human flesh as either to desert or lose, or to transfer and as
it were, contract within this frail body, the care of governing
the universe. This is the thought of men unable to see anything
but corporeal things. . . . God is great not in mass, but in might.
Hence the greatness of His might feels no straits in narrow
surroundings. Nor, if the passing word of a man is heard at
once by many, and wholly by each, is it incredible that the
abiding Word of God should be everywhere at once?*
—Saint Augustine, quoted in Thomas Aquinas

*The Lord makes his people sensible of the vanity of the present
life, by a constant proof of its miseries. Thus, that they may
not promise themselves deep and lasting peace in it, he often
allows them to be assailed by war, tumult, or rapine, or to be
disturbed by other injuries. That they may not long with too
much eagerness after fleeting and fading riches, or rest in those
which they already possess, he reduces them to want, or, at least,
restricts them to a moderate allowance, at one time by exile,
at another by sterility, at another by fire, or by other means.*
—John Calvin

MMT's insights are relatively straightforward, particularly when compared to Neoclassical economics and its abstruse mathematics. Still, as I demonstrated in my introduction, MMT frequently confounds those who encounter it. This befuddlement owes something to the school's unfamiliar and counter-hegemonic assumptions. However, both the intensity and sheer persistence of such confusion suggest that a deeper obstacle is at work. My claim, here, is that the present incomprehension surrounding neochartalism traces deep historical roots and that Liberal modernity lacks the metaphysical supports required to make sense of MMT's intervention.

This was not always so. The late medieval theology of Thomas Aquinas saw the cosmos organized around a boundless and inalienable center. Thomist metaphysics took the shape of a transcendent cascade. Thomism's boundless cascade linked dependent beings to God across great distances and did so through the Church's emphatically abstract intermediations. For many, money too took part in this transcendent cascade. Especially noteworthy are the Thomist jurists, who argued that sovereign fiscal holdings and capacities are akin to Christ's dual nature. While the jurists treated the sovereign "fisc" as an earthly and temporal body, they insisted that this fisc's underlying metaphysical structure was infinite, ubiquitous, and inalienable. Later, Thomist metaphysics were variously challenged: first by Franciscan theologians and then by Florentine humanists. The result gave rise to a distinctly modern Western metaphysics. Now taken for granted as the impassible structure of reality, these metaphysics actively reorganized the real into a decentralized, bounded, and alienable haecceity. They tethered abstraction to a contingent thisness and permitted no veritable action at a distance. As a consequence, I contend, modern metaphysics rendered care's capacious center imperceptible and money's chartalist topology illegible.

In this chapter I situate the transition from late medieval to early modern metaphysics within shifting political and economic contexts in order to rethink the metaphysical foundations of Liberal modernity for critical theory. In the scholastic models of Thomas, I recover the capacious metaphysical supports that MMT demands. With the emergence of Franciscan and humanist thought, I chart the foreclosure of these supports and critique the contracted metaphysics of mediation that come to rule modern money relations. Simultaneously, I insist that money's boundless public center does not simply vanish as it is banished from modern thought. Rather, it persists as the invisible center of caretaking in modernity. As such, money's boundless center actively structures modern appearance at the same time as its underlying topology goes undetected. Meanwhile, this topology becomes perceptible primarily as symptoms, cryptic signs indicating the repressions, contradictions, and failures that the modern metaphysics of haecceity condition.

I therefore argue that critical theory after MMT involves a double movement. It assumes a critical phenomenology grounded in money's boundless public center. Concurrently, it adopts a symptomology of care, which answers Liberal modernity's impoverished metaphysics of haecceity. With this double movement, critical theory radically expands the metaphysical capacities that condition modern political economy. It also reverses Liberal modernity's metaphysical foreclosure of care by repairing its past damages and injustices. As I show in chapter 4, critical theory's double movement is essential for uncovering the crippling limits of modernity's dialectic between money and aesthetics and for reconstituting this relation on more copious premises. Here I lay the theoretical groundwork for this critical labor by casting the origins of modern money in a wholly new light.

The Riddle of Mediation in the High Middle Ages

After 1000 AD the lives of men and women in Western Europe underwent a marked expansion in scale. Prior to this, during the first period of what we call the Middle Ages, civil wars, regular foreign invasions and raids, and the collapse of Roman imperial infrastructures contracted political and economic relations into small and relatively isolated manorial units where coin was rarely used. Manors consisted of a single castle, church, village, and surrounding farmland. Diets were meager. Marauding knights raped and pillaged. Danger hemmed in manorial life on all sides. Social relations were hierarchical, immediate, and personal. "Sheer physical survival preoccupied most people in the early Middle Ages," writes historian Steven Ozment. "The task of preserving basic social structures was paramount, and little time and treasure could be given over to the higher goals of civilization; supplying the basic physical needs of life allowed little beyond a rudimentary development of education and culture."[1]

In the centuries following the year 1000, however, the papacy authorized and helped construct a robust monetary system, allowing production to increase, violence to diminish, and social relations to widen. Centered in Rome, this system of taxation and banking arose as a political obligation to the papal center and only later grew to adopt gold and silver tokens. The result forged a vast network of production and distribution, integrating North and South, East and West under a more or less unified Christian order. Medievalist W. E. Lunt, working through freshly opened papal archives at the beginning of the twentieth century, offered a detailed account of this Church-based money system.[2] Against the prevailing Liberal historiography that imagines modern money arising from the spontaneous activities of intrepid merchants and bankers in northern Italy, Lunt argued that the late medieval system of papal finance created the political and infrastructural foundations for modern political economy. The emergence of Italian trade and banking depended upon this unrecognized foundation.

> The Roman Catholic Church, nevertheless, with an almost modern system of taxation covering all of Western Europe, furnished one of the principal forces which aided the establishment of money and credit transactions on a large scale. The changing of the sums received for taxes from money of local circulation into that of universal acceptance, the deposit and transfer of these sums, and the loans demanded by the clergy who were responsible for them stimulated the commercial and financial enterprise of the Italian banking-houses, if, indeed, their business as papal fiscal agents was not the initial cause of their transalpine activities.[3]

In Lunt's reading of the papal archive, it was the Church's European-wide system of taxation that granted locally minted currencies universal acceptance. And rather than the daring entrepreneurs and financiers celebrated and described in modern historiography, it was the papal payment system designed to service loans to the clergy that engendered commerce and banking relations from northern Italy to well beyond the Alps.

As the papal and various local money systems grew, the cloistered immediacy of manorial existence gave way to open and bustling towns ruled by guilds and other representatives of the newly influential urban middle classes. Invasions and raids subsided. The knighthood, still in many respects an important social caste, adopted a new code of chivalry, which took the edge off its violent marauding. Freshly cleared lands permitted larger and more varied agricultural yields, along with the assistance of three-field crop rotation, the heavy plough, and new upright windmills. Diets swelled. Life expectancy extended. The population nearly doubled. Silver and then gold coins began to circulate in wider spheres. Regular commercial activity and a profitable pilgrimage economy fostered geographical mobility and interactions among strangers. The Church's ongoing crusades, too, were able to expand through the technology of coinage. Wreaking havoc across the eastern Mediterranean, the crusades in turn stimulated commerce abroad, further widening the scope of Western Christendom.

Altogether, such transformations engendered what became a central enigma for the High Middle Ages: what does it mean to be interrelated at such tremendous distances? That is, more significant than the physical movements and contacts made possible by the expanding political and monetary system of the High Middle Ages were the broadened phenomenological horizon this system engendered and the riddles of mediation this distended relationality brought to the fore. Slowly the period replaced the constricted and nervous purview of manorial existence with an open, integrating, and often hubristic sense of an ever-widening Christendom. In order to make sense of this swelling horizon, Western Christendom oriented sensoria around a boundless metaphysical center and a great Chain of Being composed of God at the summit, the Universal Church as earthly authority, and a scattered laity under the care of God's Church and its dispersed community of priests. Mediation according to these metaphysics was not confined to local movements and contiguous interactions. Instead, mediation was thought to unfold as an active and dilating center, a great "body of Christ" that transmutes worldly relations through a mysterious intercessional hierarchy.

This transcendent cascade furnished the High Middle Ages with a common means for making sense of the political and economic infrastructures that mediated social relations across great distances that were not only spatial but also involved disparate languages and customs. Indeed, far from a simple or idealized theology, the era's vision of a boundless metaphysical center and all-encompassing hierarchy informed the living practices of mediation that structured social life. The audacious Gothic art and architecture of the High Middle Ages, for instance, is known for its dizzying tracery, unmoored figures, and soaring vaults. Emblematized by the period's ornate and towering cathedrals, Gothic form twists up, against, and beyond the threshold of the perceptible, suspending beholders in God's bewildering infinitude. In the same spirit, universities erected at Bologna, Paris, and Oxford, and the scholastic theologians who came to rule them, promulgated an abstract and highly intricate theology, which seems to wind variously down, around, and through Western Christendom's labyrinthine echelons of being. While the scholastics mobilized these abstract metaphysics to integrate and reconcile Christian theology with heterogeneous intellectual traditions, the universities these schoolmen occupied turned this theological system toward the more practical business of cultivating the class of lawyers, accountants, and administrators who would staff a multi-tiered European bureaucracy.

Nowhere did the riddle of mediation become more concentrated in the High Middle Ages than in the mystery of Christ's body as mediated by the Eucharist host. As early as the fourth century Gregory of Nyssa had wondered about the strange topology and causal structure suggested by the Eucharist. "How [is] it possible," he asked, "that . . . one Body, being for ever portioned to so many myriads of the faithful throughout the whole world, enters, through that portion, whole into each individual, and yet remains whole in itself?"[4] In addition to its divine and seemingly material omnipresence, the Eucharist had also long been understood as a medium of salvation. "The Eucharist both celebrated and formed the community of charity, the Church," writes historian Gary Macy.[5] For the Eucharist to prove salvific, Macy explains, it must not merely

celebrate the spirit of Christian charity. It must also conse-
crate a total life of good works oriented toward the Christian
community as a whole.

It was with the phenomenal expansion of collective existence
during the High Middle Ages that the mystery of Eucharistic
mediation and salvation took on intensified metaphysical and
political significance. Around the middle of the eleventh century,
the consecration and transubstantiation of the Eucharist became
the high point of the Catholic Mass, in addition to playing
important roles in sacred rituals for the sick and dying. In 1047,
however, Bishop Berengar of Tours stirred up controversy by
denouncing as absurd and against reason the popular belief that
Christ's body might be made physically present on countless
local altars at the same time.[6] Instead he stressed the symbolic
and memorial function of the Eucharist ritual and affirmed the
sacred significance of the blessing ritual. Hardly a novel claim in
the history of Christian theology, Berengar's argument struck
a nerve in a context in which the increasingly spectacularized
mediation of Christ's body on the altar was becoming "the
focus of all hopes and aspirations of late Medieval religion," as
Eamon Duffy describes it, and a "medium congruentissimum,"
an instrument for social communion.[7] In 1079 Pope Gregory
VII finally settled the matter in favor of Berengar's numerous
detractors. Gregory's "Eucharist Credo" made the true substance
and real presence of Christ's body in the Eucharist a matter of
official Church doctrine, inviting centuries of curious Chris-
tians to train their eyes upon this common medium in order to
witness a boundless metaphysical center realized in the flesh.

As Western Christendom ballooned into an integrated political and economic totality, the Holy Eucharist became a rich
multisensory spectacle for staging the mystery of mediation at a
distance and involving every Christian in a grand metaphysical
drama of redemption. Dramatically lit by wax lights or torches,

and often put into relief by dark curtains, the Eucharist host would appear on a high altar set removed from the congregation and, at the sound of a bell, was lifted high for all to see. Mysteriously veiled by extravagant "rood screens," the space of the altar was a distinctly sacred one, belonging to priestly authority alone. That said, "the screen itself was both a barrier and no barrier," writes Duffy. "It was not a wall but rather a set of windows, a frame for the liturgical drama, solid only to waist-height, pierced by a door wide enough for ministers and a choir to pass through and which the laity themselves might penetrate on occasions."[8] The screen thus proved as involving as it was estranging, part of a "complex and dynamic understanding of distance and proximity, concealment and exposure in the experience of the liturgy."[9] Through an ambiguous play of absence and presence, collective signification and immanent embodiment, seeing meant believing and the act of looking transformed the process of mediation into a type of transcendence. Moreover, as Duffy also makes clear, the threat of unbelief remained integral to this visual transcendence. Expressly calling out to doubters and the despairing, the Eucharist hailed a community of potential disbelievers in order to return them back to the body of Christ and community of the faithful.

As a sensuously and socially involving answer to an expanding political and economic order, the Eucharist of the High Middle Ages offers a rich model for lending shape and sense to the mystery of mediation at a distance. Unlike the model of immediate mediation that dominates the modern monetary imagination, the Eucharist makes perceptible a boundless metaphysical center and the transcendent, inexhaustible, and nonlocal co-presence this center's mediating activity implies. Let us, then, affirm the basic (and perhaps unconscious) impulses of a people striving to make sense of the mediating activity that unifies and supports them. For the mystery of Eucharistic mediation provides a way for us today to begin perceiving money's boundless omnipresence in the immanent textures of collective life.

The Angelic Doctor and the "Most Holy Fisc"

In turning the historical potential of mediation in the High Middle Ages toward present limitations, the writings of the "angelic doctor," Thomas, are indispensable. Of all the scholastic theologians, Thomas went furthest to comprehend the expansive unity of social existence during the High Middle Ages. Thomas's political theology can hardly be imported whole hog into a modern context, given the historical alterity of the medieval world and the comparatively weaker importance of money in the political order of that time. Nonetheless, Thomas's metaphysics of mediation and corresponding understanding of abstraction represent a welcomed alternative to the contracted topology of money's abstract value that has dominated the modern age.

Thomas's singular achievement, most developed in his *Summa Theologica*, was to integrate reason and revelation, nature and God, into a creative, diverse, and interdependent whole. In this way he sought to overcome the false oppositions and conflicts that preoccupied previous scholastic theology. As was the case for all scholastics, theology remained the master science for Thomas. But rather than get lost in disputes over whether faith or reason held sway in any given context, Thomas developed an *a posteriori* theology, which began from sensory experience and posited a metaphysics he thought must be true in order for the sensuous world to appear as it does. On one hand, he rejected stand-alone universals or positive essences, which would seem to determine the natural world from above. Universals are actively realized through particulars, Thomas argued, and cannot be held to subsist independently or outside of them. On the other hand, Thomas insisted that all individuated beings must be seen as having transcendental attributes. Worldly diversity emanates from an enormous and imperceptible totality, according to Thomas. Structured around an invisible boundless center and a transcendental hierarchy of interdependent beings, Thomas's metaphysics deliberately mirrored the political and economic edifice he perceived in the world around him. Finally, reason and revelation represented two means for making sense of this totality. While reason permits us to trace and assess what is perceptible in nature, revelation allows us to assay the imperceptible structure of metaphysics as a whole.

To comprehend Thomas's conception of mediation, and how he treats abstraction in particular, one must understand the Thomist account of creation. Thomas presumes a free giving God, or creator, who perpetually imparts Being unto beings *ex nihilo*. To do so, said creator actualizes what Thomas deems "prime matter," defined as a pure and inherently formless material potentiality. In creation, then, a boundless metaphysical center comes to realize prime matter's potential by way of individuated particulars. However, as Thomas makes absolutely clear, this realizing process traces a very wide movement, which hinges upon the restless activity of the center's entire transcendental cascade. The movement of creation is irreducible to locomotion through circumscribed space, Thomas argues after Aristotle. Rather, movement describes a broad transit between potentiality and actuality. This actualizing movement encompasses local movements. Yet it also necessarily transcends and perdures beyond contiguous happenstance.

In Thomas's metaphysics of creation, what *comes to be* fundamentally depends upon a large number of active and intentional agents. But the total integrated structure of things bears and supports individuation through a wide and relatively unwavering embrace. What this means is that creation permits a great deal of particularity, volition, and variability. It means that the creator greatly relies on individuated creations to perpetuate the movement of actualization. But it also means that processes of individuation remain both caught within and bounded by a thick latticework of interdependence. This dense mesh can certainly accommodate radical forms of individuation and contingency. Yet according to Thomas, it tends to shelter creation from the blows of radical particularity and the local contingencies precipitated therein.

Thomas's metaphysics of creation are crucial for explicating his account of mediation and the operations of abstraction. Mediation is precisely how creation moves potentiality into actuality in this wide and dependent sense. And abstraction is the process whereby what becomes links thing to soul and soul to thing. "The process works both ways," Thomas writes in his *Questiones Disputate de Veritate* (1256–59). "First in the direction from things to mind, corresponding to the movement of the sensitive part into the mind to reach its climax there. . . . The second direction is the soul into things, starting from mind and leading into sensitive parts."[10] But again this circuit moves *mediately*, which in Thomist metaphysics always involves passing through the universal and, with it, the center's cascading whole. Essentially, then, abstraction is neither a movement away from particulars understood as primary nor an evacuation of specificity that would otherwise remain intact. Abstraction is not a departure *from* creation; it is, rather, a part *of* creation, reaching through the universal and both ways between sensitive parts and singular things.[11]

Thomas's nuanced treatment of Eucharistic mediation is a perfect example of his conception of abstraction. In Thomas's account, the transubstantiation of the Eucharist involves two distinct yet inextricable media. First there is the local and embodied medium of the bread. Second is the "body of Christ": metaphysical medium, the meta-medium, as it were, comprising the interdependent chain of willing beings needed to actualize the transformation of localized bread into sacred host. Whereas the bread medium is wholly contained in a circumscribed location on the altar, the meta-medium that is the Christ body encompasses this localized bread within a larger movement of actualization. Involving God, Church, priest, laity, and the whole material situation of the Eucharistic ritual, Christ's body implies a complex topology whereby its mediating action at once transcends and transfigures the bread's delimited place. Thomas describes this topology in his *Summa Contra Gentiles:* "The body of Christ is not related to this place with its own dimensions as medium, so that the place need be equated to those dimensions, but His body is there with the persisting dimensions of the bread as medium, and to these the place is equated."[12]

Importantly for Thomas, Eucharistic co-presence is corporeal, not merely memorial or symbolic. Christ's body is emphatically "there" and truly transformative within localized dimensions. That said, its thereness is not present in the conventionally understood sense. Instead, Thomas characterizes the movement of Christ's body into the Eucharist as "sacramentally present." As we read in his *Summa Theologica,*

Christ's body is not in this sacrament in the same way as a body is in a place, which by its dimensions is commensurate with the place; but in a special manner which is proper to this sacrament. Hence we say that Christ's body is upon many altars, not as in different places, but "sacramentally": and thereby we do not understand that Christ is there only as in a sign, although a sacrament is a kind of sign; but that Christ's body is here after a fashion proper to this sacrament.[13]

Here Thomas defines Eucharistic presence as a material and meaningful sacramental presence, while refusing symbolic reductionism. In so doing, Thomas is able to account for the material body's contingent comings and goings. But he also makes perceptible the transcendent meta-medium that equally imparts shape and value to embodied space.

Above all, what for Thomas separates Eucharistic mediation from direct material mediation is its constitutive *inalienability*. Through the Eucharist sacrament, God requires mortal assistance to carry out what he deems "the work of our redemption."[14] Indeed, the Eucharist ritual enacts the Passion of God's self-sacrifice for the salvation of those indebted to the order of divine creation. According to Thomas, however, God's apparent self-dispossession does not evacuate any one or thing from the center of creation. Instead, Eucharistic mediation constitutes an inalienable donation or surplus, which derives from nowhere other than the expansive cascade of interdependency that makes up the expansive body of Christendom. This is why Thomas categorically rejects appeals to the physics of locomotion for understanding Eucharistic mediation.

> Now it is evident that Christ's body does not begin to be present in this sacrament by local motion. First of all, because it would follow that it would cease to be in heaven: for what is moved locally does not come anew to some place unless it quit the former one. Secondly, because every body moved locally passes through all intermediary spaces, which cannot be said here. Thirdly, because it is not possible for one movement of the same body moved locally to be terminated in different places at the one time, whereas the body of Christ under this sacrament begins at the one time to be in several places.[15]

As Thomas explains, Eucharistic mediation embroils participants in a sacred and inherently inalienable medium. In opposition to locomotive matter, this medium never ceases to remain complete and intact. It need not physically pass through intermediary spaces to arrive at a destination. It comes into being, not in a movement *from* here *to* there but, rather, all at once and at geographically dispersed locations.

While Thomas discusses money in relation to his metaphysics, he never connected such mediations to the fiscal instrument that serves as money's infrastructural backbone. However, nothing prevents us from doing so for a contemporary monetary imagination unable to reckon with its own processes of mediation and abstraction. Liberal modernity has become incapable of seeing the boundless and inalienable meta-medium that organizes nearly every other form of mediation in collective life. However, Thomas's political theology provides a means to develop a new carnal knowledge of the way it always already engenders the interdependent totality we inhabit. To embrace Thomist mediation today does not necessitate reviving a pre-modern, hierarchical, or anthropocentric cosmology in which we hallucinate "the eyes of the universe telescopically focused from all sides on [our] thoughts and actions," as Nietzsche once quipped.[16] To the contrary, it requires learning to perceive the whole mystery of salvation contained in the monetary relation and, for the time being anyway, placing the care of this decentered and fragile planet in money's limitless and inalienable center.

Although never fully manifested in Thomas's own writings, the late medieval jurists who inherited his political theology offer a model for turning Thomas's metaphysics of mediation toward a fresh vision of the public purse. Dismissed in a footnote in the first volume of Marx's *Capital*, and left largely underdeveloped in Desan's *Making Money*, the peculiar metaphysics of the late medieval fiscal instrument have been most thoroughly explored by Ernst Kantorowicz in his well-known book *The King's Two Bodies: A Study in Medieval Political Theology* (1958). In chapters dedicated to late medieval juridical treatises, Kantorowicz makes plain the influence of Thomist metaphysics on the figure of the sovereign "fisc" or "fiscus" and devotes dozens of pages to elaborating what he calls the "budding fiscal 'theology'" of thirteenth- and fourteenth-century Europe.[17]

Kantorowicz begins by unpacking what becomes a seemingly strange, yet apparently common juridical comparison of the age between "Christus" and "fiscus." "The jurists would talk about the *sacratissimus fiscus* or *fiscus sanctissimus*, 'the most holy fisc,' a phrase having a curious ring only in modern ears," he writes.[18] Dwelling particularly on the texts of twelfth-century English jurist Herni de Bracton, Kantorowicz explicates how the late medieval sacralization of the fisc corresponds to a proto-modern political differentiation between a perishable corporeal ruler and the inalienable office of sovereignty: what he terms the "king's two bodies." "Things pertaining to the king's peace and jurisdiction were 'things quasi holy, *res quasi sacrae*,'" Kantorowicz expounds, "which could no more be alienated than could *res sacrae* pertaining to the Church. Those things 'quasi holy' were 'things public' existing for some common utility of the realm, such as the preservation of justice and peace."[19] In these juridical texts, the purse and property of a living sovereign might be legally subjected to dispossession and estrangement. Yet the sacred fisc adhered to a suprapersonal and incorporeal sovereignty, held to be as untouchable and inalienable as the body of Christ.

Thomas's political theology played an instrumental role in the fisc's sacralization and, with this, shaped the embryonic development of what would later become the secular state. In particular, Kantorowicz argues, Thomas expanded the meaning of "corpus mysticum," which had been associated with Eucharistic real presence and mystical body of Christ, to signify a proto-secular "juristic abstraction," an "organism acquiring social and corporational functions."[20] Indeed, the fingerprints of Thomas's mystical body shape the terms late medieval jurists used to capture the essence of the fisc's perplexing ontology. The essential being or nature of the fisc was identified as the "soul of the state" and deemed to be "abstract" or "fictitious."[21] In terms of space, the fisc was characterized as ubiquitous, as "everywhere and ever present," while its temporality was regarded as "immortal," existing "beyond time" as such.[22] Often the link between the fisc and the Christian God was explicit. "The fisc is omnipresent," wrote the fourteenth-century Italian jurist Baldus de Ubaldis, "and in that, therefore, the fisc resembles God."[23] As Baldus's language of comparison indicates, however, the fisc's legal construction qua divine also presupposed its difference from, even opposition to, the boundless inalienability of the divinity.

"Therewith there emerges that seemingly weird antithesis or parallelism of *Christus* and *Fiscus* to which hitherto little or no attention has been paid," Kantorowicz concludes.[24] Countering this epistemic vacuum, he suggests that this *Christus-Fiscus* duality harbors still untold historical secrets, calling it "a central problem of political thought in the period of transition from mediaeval to modern times."[25] In what follows I answer Kantorowicz's call in a manner that modern thought's subsequent reduction of ontology prevented him from perceiving. Here I propose a wholly new account of the shift from the late medieval to early modern period. I lay bare the metaphysics of haecceity that came to constrain and repress money's boundless public center and the symptomatic spectacle of disintegration that has prevented the money relation from appearing otherwise.

Things Fall Apart

Thomas's political theology flourished and spread throughout Western Christendom in the centuries following his death. During the same period, however, this metaphysical structure came under attack from two different directions. Franciscan theologians and Italian humanists began to dismantle Thomism's centered metaphysical scaffolding and wide mediating cascade. Instead, Western European thought adopted a decentered metaphysics of haecceity, or thisness, which contracted mediation's locus, while wishing to expand its field of action. Deeming political and theological hierarchies contingent, and non-contiguous activity at a distance illusory, this new European metaphysics posited a contractual, or "covenantal," basis for mediation, forged through contacts between finite beings and a decentered almighty God. Woven imperceptibly into this relatively well-understood transformation is the untold origin of modern money as we have inherited it from Liberal political economy. To be sure, money appears obliquely and sometimes only tangentially in this changing and rather heterogeneous philosophical discourse. However, the break with Thomism was not only profoundly motivated by crises of political economy; its reduction of mediation to haecceity also constructed a metaphysical background, a historical mise-en-scène, which would make money's boundless public center imperceptible and harden the monetary relation into a delimited and disposable particular.

Whereas European life was relatively stable and prosperous until around the middle of the thirteenth century, mounting problems gave way to full blown disasters by the fourteenth century. The late thirteenth century brought increased social instability and confusion regarding the loci of political and economic authority. Local rulers, including the emperor and the French and English crowns, challenged the papacy in a long series of battles over taxation. Political friction and theological disputes forced the pope and his administrative apparatus to relocate several times until settling in Avignon. As money's influence over political life grew, urban existence turned increasingly toward relatively short and unstable contracts, with little fiscal support provisioned for the population as a whole. Riddled by un- and underemployment, insufficient collective purchasing power, and worker unrest, towns became associated with increasingly powerful middle classes, and money came to emblematize the ruination of traditional governance and long-term commitments. Thus, in the course of this multi-tiered fight for power, the warring parties recognized a shared political and economic totality. Yet in battling over who would ultimately represent and control this totality, late thirteenth-century Europe variously misrecognized, debilitated, and undermined the metaphysical center that supported Christendom as a whole.

In the early fourteenth century Western Christendom's fracturing edifice gave out from below. An exceptionally warm period in Western Europe was disrupted by what has been called a "Little Ice Age." Crops failed, livestock perished, and minimal food surpluses quickly vanished. Production collapsed. Scarcity drove prices through the roof. Landholders struggled to shore up their position. Malnutrition and disease reverberated throughout the social order. In 1347 Genoese trading vessels loaded with grotesque-looking bodies docked at Messina in Sicily. The disease they carried became the Bubonic Plague, which would kill a third of the European population and ravage the entire Eurasian land mass. Throughout the period, ruling authorities turned ever more unruly. The papacy declared absolute authority over Western Christendom. The Holy Roman Empire responded with its own total claims to power. The One Hundred Years' War saw French monarchal authority pushed back by Burgundian dukes. Increasingly empowered landed gentry squeezed greater concessions from the English crown. Finally, in recovering from famine and plague, elites passed maximum wage laws and levied heavy taxes on the poor, giving rise to ongoing worker and peasant rebellions.

As a result, the capacious center and widening purviews of the High Middle Ages variously contracted and hardened around immanent power struggles, contingent contracts, and the immediate demands of physical survival. Rather than retreating into dispersed and isolated communities, however, Western European elites paradoxically cultivated the period's symptomatic phenomenological constrictions into a new metaphysical system, subordinating mediation to haecceity within a totality that only continued to enlarge. Hence, while Western Christendom's abandonment of the political center precipitated a debilitating phenomenological contraction, social and cultural authorities elevated this symptomatic evacuation into a positive way of knowing and perceiving that banished money's boundless public center as it came to subsume modern life.

The assault on Thomism came from two primary sources. The first was the Franciscan theology of Scotus and Ockham. Scotus and Ockham wrote from within the scholastic tradition. However, in contrast to Thomas, who belonged to the Dominican Order aligned with the papacy, Scotus and Ockham emerged from the Church's Franciscan Order, known for its insistence on apostolic poverty and implicit denunciation of clerical power and riches. In late thirteenth- and early fourteenth-century narratives and iconography Saint Francis was depicted as the mortal who had come closest to being with Jesus. Francis achieved this proximity by renouncing his allegiance to a wealthy cloth merchant father, relinquishing his patrimony and worldly possessions, and devoting himself unreservedly to moving nearer to God. The Francis story's dramatic trade-off between an earthly and heavenly father and emphatic stripping down of divine mediation not only became guiding tropes for Scotus and Ockham's metaphysics but also took on a new and contradictory intensity in its valorization of austerity.

Writing at a moment of encroaching political and economic instability, Scotus (1266–1308) and Ockham (1287–1347) refused Aquinas's commitment to a centralized metaphysical hierarchy as well as the angelic doctor's understanding of mediation as involving an all-encompassing mesh of interdependent beings. To the contrary, they asserted the metaphysical primacy of what Scotus termed "haecceitas," an omnipotent thisness that the Franciscan theologians held to be the site of divine mediation and the source from which all individuated beings stem. Scotus and Ockham vehemently disagreed on many matters. However, both thinkers rejected the Thomist vision of creation in which the universal draws out individuated beings from prime matter. Rejecting the Thomist vision of creation, Scotus and Ockham saw creation binding form and matter together through the third term of haecceity and realizing God's potency via a constitutive thisness. On this reasoning, no tremendous scaffolding mediates the passage from Being to beings over great distances since, as Ockham puts it, "prime matter and substantial form are related to place immediately."[26] For both Scotus and Ockham, God individuates being proximately, and no beings exist outside haecceity's immediate grasp.

With this topological rupture, Scotus's and Ockham's metaphysics upped the ante on Saint Francis's celebrated abandonment of worldly possessions and on his intimacy with the divine. Recall that Francis merely renounced his worldly father, exchanging earthly belongings for a heavenly father who exists beyond the basic infrastructures that organize collective life. In the case of Franciscan theology, by contrast, Scotus and Ockham vociferously denounced the necessary mediatorial role played by the papal father and Universal Church. They then wholly externalized the ground of being to a decentered center that promises close contact with an omnipresent God. With this, I argue, Scotus and Ockham turned Western metaphysics irreversibly *inside out.* They not only shifted being's center of gravity to a profoundly decentered field of existence. They also fashioned an alternative image of immanence, which encompassed the centralized infrastructures they deemed unnecessary under an all-powerful and newly decentered interior. The Franciscans' inside-out topology thereby stripped the thick imperceptible mesh of Thomas's interdependent hierarchy of any essential reality. In its place, they installed a ubiquitous haecceity that recognizes no mediating center and organizes being through immanent individuations.

The Franciscans' inside-out metaphysics forever changed Western thought's basic assumptions, problems, and aims. For one thing, Franciscan metaphysics fundamentally transformed the structure of causality. Decrying the overriding determinism they attributed to Thomas's totalizing metaphysics, Scotus and Ockham affirmed a radical contingency that derived from being's essential contiguity. If being hinges at the decentered joints of a proximate contiguity, cause and effect can then become unhinged from the securing mesh of Thomas's centralized interdependent architecture. The result allowed Scotus and Ockham to develop a voluntaristic understanding of causality in which God and mortals might freely choose the order of being from anywhere at all.

Upon the basis of this voluntarist causality, meanwhile, Scotus and Ockham came to unhinge the underlying metaphysics of mediation, signification, and abstraction. In their hands mediation was reimagined as a temporary covenant between an intentional agent and an external referent in the world. From here they transfigure signification into a conventional and largely nominalist relation, which must in some way adequately approximate external referents. Lastly, this voluntarist causality obliterated Thomas's two-way process of abstraction that tethers being to the center. In opposition to Thomist abstraction, the

Franciscans anchored abstraction in being's immanent this-ness. Like a long shadow at dusk, abstraction might stretch well beyond circumscribed being. Indeed, in a universe in which presumably anything is conceivable, such an adumbration might extend indefinitely. But in Franciscan metaphysics, infinitude is a function of haecceity, and abstraction remains bounded by haecceity, such that processes of abstraction can only project as far as a contiguous thisness permits.

It is no accident that Franciscan metaphysics spread in tandem with the political and economic unruliness of the late thirteenth and early fourteenth century. Their vanishing center and con-tracted relationality are deeply symptomatic of the period's imploding political infrastructure and phenomenological con-strictions. As symptom, moreover, Franciscan haecceity seems only to reify the experience of the money relation during late thirteenth and fourthteenth centuries. Yet to apprehend the full significance of this historical indicator, we must read it as a riddling symptom of the political center it represses. Above all, this means tracing its contradictory metaphysics, not as an abstract description of an extant reality but, rather, as an index of a historically specific configuration of the center and as a catastrophic failure of care.

The most striking contradiction of Franciscan haecceity is the fact that it expressly negates the contingent monetary contract its metaphysical structure symptomatically affirms. Remember, the Franciscans were a mendicant order of friars, who relinquished worldly possessions and railed against the Church's largesse and papal participation in political and economic life.[27] Franciscan haecceity represents an effort to undermine the Thomist meta-physics that underpinned the Church's position as the center of political economy and ultimately to escape the difficulties of monetary mediation. But the real key for interpreting haecceity's symptomology involves uncovering its hidden inner structure:

what in my introduction I called the *spectacle of disintegration* that results from the metaphysics of thisness.

Symptoms are typically "overdetermined," Freud tells us, meaning that they admit multiple and seemingly unrelated figures that nonetheless configure a single traumatic compulsion. I count a minimum of *three* distinct figures of disintegration that unconsciously sabotage as well as drive the Franciscan metaphysics of haecceity. Considered together, these figures bespeak an unconscious demand for care that their turn to haecceity represses. The first figure most fully reveals the repressed demand for care that unconsciously organizes the Franciscan affirmation of haecceity. While Scotus and Ockham conceive of haecceity as an Oedipal struggle against the allegedly unfree determinations of the papal father and Thomist Church, they continuously complain that Thomas's insistence upon God's own interdependent position in the order of beings threatens to diminish the all-powerful God they construct as an alternative metaphysical ground. The Franciscans perpetually conjure the dissolution of God's hyper-potent haecceity, not because they avow that God can be diminished but, rather, in an effort to fend against those they accuse of alienating His apparently inalienable might. Yet in doing so, the Franciscan appeal to thisness betrays an unconscious longing for the boundless interdependent center it purports heroically to abandon.

A second figure of disintegration in Franciscan metaphysics is their insistence on stripping oneself bare of earthly possessions. This figure is equally contradictory and mirrors the structure of the first. Continually reenacting the impoverishment of individuated experience wrought by the metaphysics of haecceity, this thinning of experience promises a stronger and more abundant ground for being that lies beyond the excesses of papal mediation and the anxieties of political economy. But in truth, this incessant phenomenological diminishment not only hardens the sensorium against haecceity's disintegrating effects but also deepens the poisonous contraction of metaphysics that arises from the era's impoverishment of worldly existence.

Finally, the third figure of disintegration that riddles Franciscan haecceity concerns how its radical affirmation of a contingent deity unmoors the history of Western thought that follows. As Ozment writes of Ockham's influence,

> By dwelling so intently on God's will rather than his being, Ockham created the conditions for a new spiritual anxiety— not the possible nonexistence of God, but the suspicion that he might not keep his word; that he could not be depended upon to do as he promised; that the power behind all things may ultimately prove to be untrustworthy and unfriendly; that God, in a word, might be a liar. Not God's existence, but his goodness; not the rationality of faith, but the ability to trust God—these became major spiritual problems.[28]

The unnerving specter raised by Franciscan haecceity is that the contingent covenant that is supposed to bind God to mortals may very well be untrustworthy; that God might willfully abandon individuals; and that, at a moment's notice, He may deliberately choose for persons to fall into ruination. Therefore, while the Franciscans insist upon the inalienability of their omnipotent thisness, the figures of disintegration that haunt Franciscan haecceity index a leakage at the heart of their metaphysics. More than a mere failure of reasoning, this leakage unconsciously calls out to the boundless center for a care that Scotus and Ockham consciously forsake.

The Franciscans' negation of the monetary relation prepares the metaphysical groundwork for a distinctly modern money form structured around a hemorrhaging haecceity that Franciscan metaphysics make intelligible. However, modernity's eventual reduction of money to an alienable thisness is a profoundly dialectical process. While it begins with the Franciscan negation of political and economic mediation, it culminates with the ambivalent affirmation of money in the writings of the Renaissance humanists. The resulting synthesis gave birth to a distinctly modern monetary instrument, which would be lauded for its capacities to increase collective and personal wealth but also taken for an agent of destruction and therefore a source of constant anxiety and ambivalence. To comprehend this dialectization of modern money, I turn to the political economy of early modern Florence and to the rise of humanistic traditions.

Blood Spurt to the Stars

At least since the publication of Jacob Burckhardt's *The Civilization of the Renaissance in Italy* (1860), Renaissance Florence has been described as the birthplace of Western secular humanism and, in a sense, as the cradle of modern commerce and culture. This tradition has been equally acclaimed and decried for its self-aggrandizing sense of the individual prince, merchant, banker, intellectual, and artist. It has been recognized for the emergence of self-conscious and explicitly anti-theological understandings of commercial associations, technological know-how, and political power. It has been noted for its natural and expansive vision of the cosmos organized around an omnipresent, ever-changing, and decidedly decentered God. The polymath and German cardinal Nicholas de Cusa offered the most explicit articulation of this emerging Renaissance cosmology. "It is impossible for the world machine to have this sensible earth, air, fire, or anything else for a fixed and immovable center," he wrote. "Therefore, the world machine will have, one might say, its center everywhere and its circumference nowhere, for its circumference and center is God, who is everywhere and nowhere."[29]

Developed by Hans Baron's *The Crisis of the Italian Renaissance* (1955) and variously debated by countless others, this Burckhard-tian story has long imagined the difficulties and aspirations of early modern Florence as the rudiments of Western modernity, even if scholars debate the precise extent to which the Renais-sance can be seen as distinct from either the preceding High Middle Ages or the modern era that would follow. But whatever the Florentine Renaissance's precise periodicity, the scholarly consensus is that it constitutes something like a template for making sense of what it means to inhabit a decentered and con-tingent world that is predominantly mediated by money. I agree that the Florentine moment marks a crucial origin and turning point in the history of modernity. However, in approaching this historical wellspring from the perspective of MMT's neochartalist understanding of monetary mediation, and doing so specifi-cally with an eye toward the *fiscal* politics that shaped the era, Renaissance Florence begins to look like the birthplace of the modern Liberal money form, conceived as a private, decentered, and alienable thisness. By training the senses to perceive only what is proximate, substantial, and active, humanistic meth-ods foreclosed the possibility of perceiving money's boundless public center and prevented future generations from seeing abstraction as the source of collective salvation. Humanists noto-riously ridiculed the likes of Scotus and Ockham for obfuscating abstractions and hypocritical asceticism. As will become clear, however, the humanist project fundamentally converged with the Franciscan metaphysics and economics it opposed in that it, too, reduced mediation to a contingent thisness, while fabulating a new understanding of money as a private and alienable thing.

Recounted by orthodox economists, Marxists, and myriad scholars of the early modern period, the political economy of the Florentine Renaissance has not yet been properly treated from a chartalist perspective.[30] Seen through the lens of MMT, however, it becomes possible to construct a chartalist account of the Florentine political economy from the facts that have been made available. Over the course of the Florentine Renaissance—that is, from the dawn of the fourteenth century to the middle of the sixteenth century—the political economy of Florence was structured by perpetual want, instability, and crisis. Throughout the period Florence increasingly centralized and bureaucratized the city-state under a new regime of impersonal law.[31] It became a major financial and commercial center across Italy, Europe, and beyond. It saw lavish expenditures on secular and religious institutions as well as the arts. However, the political economy of the Florentine city-state as a whole was wildly underfunded, financially insecure, and torn by class division.

The violent instability of Florence's political economy owed in part to fluctuating currency values, cutthroat competition, worker suppression including maximum wage laws and the denial of recognition for working-class trades, explosive population growth, rampant disease, increasingly costly wars, and the general unruliness of a hurried urbanization. However, as any student of MMT would immediately detect, Florence's recurring volatility resulted primarily from inadequate and poorly distributed public expenditures and, specifically, from the fact that government spending was artificially constrained by the finitude of tax and bond revenues. Of course, it would be ahistorical and disingenuous to demand that the Florentines ought to have "known better" in what was surely an opaque and rapidly shifting milieu. Still, it would be equally ahistorical to overlook the conspicuous absence of Bracton's boundless and inalienable fisc in the Florentine context and similarly simple-minded to reduce the historicity of Florence's political economy to the period's conscious intentions and extant beliefs.

MMT helps us see the true structural fault lines of Renaissance Florence's political economy. What is important to understand is that, despite the city-state's ongoing confrontations with the papacy and fervent proclamations of its Tuscan *libertas*, Florence's fiscal capacities remained legally and institutionally wedded to the papal financial system—that is, at least until 1380, a moment to which I shall soon return. As a principality in this system, Florence relied on the papacy to underwrite and enforce the city-state's bimetallist monetary order and myriad debt obligations. At the center of the Florentine monetary order was the Monte, or "mountain," the limited public debt instrument designed to fund the city-state's fiscal expenditures through bond sales. The trouble was that since its founding in 1347, the Monte had radically restricted public financing, creating systemic unemployment, insufficient aggregate spending power, and a constant need for insecure private borrowing. Also, the amount of interest-paying bonds (*preztante*) furnished by the Monte skyrocketed throughout the period, diverting as much as two thirds of Florentine tax revenues from the public coffers.[32] As a consequence, the Monte became for Florence an ersatz fiscal instrument. Intrinsically weak and miserable at allocating debt where and when it was needed, Monte interest payments nonetheless countered the slack in direct fiscal spending and functioned as a structurally necessary institution for supporting everything from government infrastructures to art production to marriage dowries. Thus, while Renaissance Florence was surely inundated by numerous political, social, and material problems, nearly all of these difficulties were mediated by what historian David Herlihy has called the city-state's "fiscal pauperism" and by an unruly public debt system, which proved incapable of preserving either justice or peace.[33]

Florence during the Renaissance era held an exceptional status as a powerhouse of European banking, industry, and commerce. In comparison to other commercial centers in Tuscany, the Veneto, and Flanders, Florence's crisis-ridden fiscal and public debt system was fairly typical, even if the Florentines experienced more intense contractions and expansions than did other cities. What makes Renaissance Florence exceptional, however, is the fact that, as a result of a protracted war with the papacy, the city-state consciously disembedded its fiscal apparatus and public debt system from the papal monetary system through which it emerged.

Florence's devastating "War of Eight Saints" (1375–78) against Pope Gregory XI came about when an English mercenary, John Hawkwood, marched an army of papal soldiers toward Florence and demanded 130,000 florins for a peace pact that would call off his troops. Eight elite Florentines formed a war council in order to meet Hawkwood's demands. Levying taxes on the clergy to pay for the expense, these "Eight Saints" promptly prepared Florence for a war against Pope Gregory. The battle would be financed through forced taxation and the sale of church property, which, in David S. Peterson's judgment, represents "the most extensive liquidation of an ecclesiastical patrimony carried out anywhere in Europe before the Reformation."[34] Gregory responded with a papal interdict, which denied the administration of all sacraments except baptism, conformation, and penance; forbade priests from participating in public religion processions; and withheld the consecrated host from being viewed by anyone in Florence. And this all proceeded in the midst of a four-year "Ciompi" workers rebellion, which, in the summer of 1378, led to a short-lived Ciompi government that attempted to guarantee work for all and eliminate the elitist Monte structure. The war was brutal, drained city resources, and proved a constant source of civic conflict and resentment. Military clashes lasted for only three years. But these military skirmishes were overshadowed by protracted legal and financial battles, which, as Peterson tells it, "precipitated a constitutional struggle that lasted . . . to the mid-fifteenth century."[35]

A key outcome of the 1380 peace settlement between Florence and the new Pope Urban VI would permanently transform monetary relations between Florence, the papacy, and the Florentine clergy. In exchange for pledging allegiance to the papacy and promising the pope 130,000 florins in reparations payments, the Florentine city-state won de facto political autonomy from the Universal Church and de jure independence for its monetary system. Tragically, however, rather than declaring the boundlessness and inalienability of its freshly won fisc, the Florentine city-state affirmed its fundamental boundedness to finite tax and bond revenues and therefore continued to suffer from financial crises and social unrest.

More profoundly, the accord fundamentally inverted the political and economic relationship between Florence and the papal financial system in a manner that rendered popes and the Church increasingly dependent upon Florence's finite Monte and tax system. Peterson outlines the far-reaching consequences of this inverted relation:

> Beforehand, Florence had needed the papacy to serve as the legal guarantor of the Monte. Now the relationship of dependence was reversed. Popes from Urban VI (1338–89) to Gregory XII (1406–15) relied on (meager) Florentine indemnity payments to keep their finances afloat, and after the schism Popes Martin V (1417–31) to Eugenius IV (1431–47) both sought to bolster papal finances by investing heavily in the Monte. Through their Monte shares, the financial interests of the local Florentine clergy also became tied to those of the Florentine state. . . . The Monte and [tax system] thus became the basic bureaucratic instruments whereby Florence circumscribed, supervised, and manipulated the financial operations of the church within its expanding territorial state.[36]

Reversing the dependency between Florence and the papacy, the War of the Eight Saints turned the basic political (if not also metaphysical) underpinnings of the European monetary system inside out. Whereas before the war Florence struggled under the yoke of a boundless and inalienable papal medium to which it had insufficient access, after the war both Florence and the papacy both tethered their very subsistence to a brutally finite Florentine *libertas.*

Renaissance humanism and art performed significant and hitherto unexamined roles in developing new phenomenological bases for the paradoxically finite and explosive field of mediation that defined Florence's troubled political economy. Emerging well before the War of the Eight Saints and enduring long thereafter, Renaissance humanism and art constructed a general *topos* of mediation, which granted ontological weight and meaning only to sensuous bodies and actions, while increasingly denying actuality to abstract figures and relations at a distance. From this generalized *topos* of mediation, Florentines would come to dialectize the Franciscan rejection of money as an alienable thisness and, instead, affirm the monetary relation both as advantageous for the common good and as an agent of worldly dissolution. Here, I wish to address the humanist contribution to this uneasy project, while saving my analysis of Renaissance art for the final chapter.

Humanism first emerged in the northern Italian peninsula. As Ronald G. Witt has persuasively argued, a deepening split between ecclesiastical and lay notaries who conspicuously specialized in contracts saw the latter group develop an appreciation for the ancients and begin to imitate ancient Latin style.[37] Later, well-known figures such as Petrarch (1304–74), Lorenzo Valla (1407–57), and Erasmus of Rotterdam (1466–1536) added to this tradition a taste for ancient rhetoric and adopted a classical ethos of self-fashioning and the pursuit of a pleasing and virtuous life. The humanists were both anti-scholastic and anti-philosophical. Favoring enlivening actions and practical forms of speaking, learning, and knowing, they rejected the apparent sterility of scholastic logic. They ridiculed the lack of feeling they detected in philosophy's tedious abstractions. The world of the humanists was one of public engagement, common sense, and bodies in motion. It was a natural and dynamic world, which demanded a grounded and variable prose. To this end the humanists crafted a style of ancient Latin prose suited for describing a particular, embodied, and shifting reality. In opposition to the comparatively flat, vernacularized Latin used by Thomas and the scholastics, humanist writers wrote in complex periodic sentences that exploited suspended meanings, paradoxes, and irony. They did so in a pure classical idiom distilled from the authors of the late Roman Republic and early Empire. In all, it was the puzzling and invigorating pleasure of language's proximity to the world that proved central to humanist style. This enjoyment also accounts for humanists' zealous commitment to philological research and translation, which extended their desire for intimate contact with the real to the past they so adored.

Since from the humanist perspective the real is grounded, animated, and centerless, money, too, appears in humanist writings as a proximate, fluctuating, and decentered thisness. Indeed, Valla despised the juridical arguments of Baldus and Accursius (1182–1263), who explicitly likened the fisc to the boundlessness and inalienability of God.[38] But there is nothing like a unified humanist philosophy of money, and deliberately so. Still, the desires and tensions that structure the humanist approach to monetary matters come to the fore in On Avarice (1428), a well-known dialogue by humanist scholar, papal secretary, and chancellor of Florence, Poggio Bracciolini (1380–1459).[39] In general, the dialogue treats money as a moral problem and situates it within a directly embodied and emphatically anti-Thomist social reality. "The most original aspect of *On Avarice*," wrote the French scholar Christian Bec, "resides in its identification of morality with the real, with existence, not utopia but, on the contrary, grounded in an acute consciousness of the living forces of the economy and contemporary society."[40]

Reducing the monetary relation to a grounded decentered process, *On Avarice* frames the question of money's moral horizon in terms of individual and familial pursuits of wealth. Specifically, it dialectically stages two opposite viewpoints. One is represented by the voices of "da Montepulciano" and "Andrea of Constantinople," who morally condemn money making as debauchery and as both private and public catastrophes. By contrast, a single speaker named "Antonio Loschi" speaks on behalf of monetary greed. But Loschi makes the case for avarice by touting money's greater advantages for communal and civic life. For without the avaricious, Loschi pronounces, "every splendor, every refinement, every ornament would be lacking. No one would build churches or colonnades; all artistic activity would cease, and confusion would result in our lives and in public affairs if everyone were satisfied with only enough for himself."[41] Loschi's extreme position is not given the final word in *On Avarice*. Instead, the text's play between contrasting positions dramatizes a complex dialectical embrace of monetary relations, laboring to involve readers in the social quandary of money. By turns enlivening and unsettling, receptive and censorious, *On Avarice*'s drama charges readers with the morally hazardous task of affirming money's various private and public uses, while avoiding its anti-social and apparently destructive underbelly.

All indications suggest that the same fraught dialectic colored Florentine relations with money more broadly and that humanist pedagogy was a central player in shaping the moral life of money within a growing merchant and bureaucratic class.[42] As Juliann M. Vitullo and Diane Wolfthal have argued, "Merchants and humanists . . . focused on the importance of using money and household possessions wisely and of teaching their sons a profession rather than how to simply make money. They understood the importance of depicting themselves and their offspring as fruitful, industrious citizens whose labor and investments benefited the entire community, rather than as sterile, avaricious usurers who hoarded the wealth for themselves."[43] Not every humanist proved equally comfortable with this project, however, reflecting lingering doubts and anxieties about the place of money in Florentine life. Erasmus was especially vocal about what he took to be money's essential corruptness and insecurity: "But tell me most foolish of men . . . what purpose do you think your money serves? . . . It cannot rid your mind of gnawing worries, it cannot drive off, or protect your body, from illness and discomfort, much less death. . . . It guarantees that you are always in want."[44]

Michelangelo (1475–1564), that most Florentine of Florentines, gave quintessential expression to a common humanist lament against papal profligacy and aggression in a sonnet titled, "On Rome in the Pontificate of Julius II."[45] Echoing similar formulations by Petrarch two centuries earlier, the sonnet envisions the corrupting role of money in the papacy as a spectacle of bodily hemorrhaging and semiological deception.[46] It begins by portraying Church officials "mak[ing] helms and swords from chalices" for commerce and war. It denounces the financing of these temporal endeavors through the desecration of holy vessels and the letting of its liquids. "The blood of Christ is now sold by the quart."[47] "Christ pours out pity from his heart," Michelangelo assures readers.[48] "But let him come no more into the streets," he warns, "since it would make his blood spurt to the stars."[49]

From the Franciscan negation of money to the ambivalent humanist synthesis, the spectacle of disintegration that surrounds the early modern money relation registers real injustices and genuine demands for care—even if mostly articulated by elites. However, I insist that the *form* of this spectacle in no way corresponds to the reality it wishes to bring near. With unreflected investment in a disintegrating here-and-now, such spectacles are symptoms of an emerging blind spot in the modern phenomenology of mediation: one that is incapable of perceiving the boundless public abstraction that organizes production and distribution at a large scale. Instead of reckoning with the ways an inalienable abstraction mediates interdependence at a distance, this phenomenology reduces mediation to a leaking vessel. In doing so, it tragically misses the mark of the mediator it seeks. The feelings of evacuation and dissolution that drive this phenomenology compress distant space into near space and contract money into a deceptive thisness, which can never be co-present everywhere at once. For this reason, I submit, the unnerving pulsations that animate Florentine money's fugitive haecceity are responsible for turning the modern phenomenology of money inside out.

Over time the pulse of Florentine money's transient thisness became the pulse of modernity itself. Vertiginous, dispersive, and disintegrating, the rhythms of haecceity furnished an encroaching modernity with a rudimentary metaphysical schema that would see money and mediation as contiguous and contingent while growing blind to the boundless public abstraction that actually conditions modernity's hazards and potentials. The Protestant Reformation radicalized the metaphysics of haecceity to reorganize wholly the political economy of Western Europe. Liberal modernity made haecceity king by imagining social reality variously as an abstract covenant that unfolds through immediate associations. Marxist materialism would adopt the same twofold ontology. However, against Liberal apologies for private commerce, Marxism grounded the real in a disintegrating haecceity and made this haecceity the basis of its many metaphoric appeals.

In the meantime the modern project of the aesthetic arose in opposition to this volatile background. Whereas money seemed to contract and dissolve sensory experience, the aesthetic sphere sought to expand and secure a modern sensorium haunted by incipient disintegration. In the final chapter of this book I reassess the modern aesthetic project in terms of haecceity's epochal seizure of money and mediation. To do so, I return to the historical emergence of perspectivalism in Renaissance Florence, where haecceity first overtakes the visual field. First, I uncover the secret of modern aesthetics within the history of this form's gravitropic embrace. Next, I critique the violent return of such aesthetics in neoliberal action-adventure media. Finally, I argue that in order to overcome neoliberal privation and actualize MMT's redemptive potential, we must relinquish the comforts of gravitropic media and embrace the pleasures of abstraction across monetary and formal spheres.

4

Allegories of the Aesthetic

There's that word again: heavy. Why are things so heavy in the future? Is there a problem with the Earth's gravitational pull?
—Doctor Emmett Brown

Theory is undertheorized. Either everything is abstract, or nothing is.
—Charles Bernstein

"No concept is more fundamental to modernity than the aesthetic," writes Geoffrey Galt Harpham, "that radiant globe of material objects and attitudes."[1] The aesthetic, in Harpham's view, "gathers into itself and focuses norms and notions crucial to . . . an enlightened culture."[2] Against the disaffections of bourgeois political economy, the aesthetic promises a kind of secular salvation: a redeemed modernity that is replete, diverse, empathic, and whole. The manifest impossibility of this promise has led critics such as Harpham to regard the aesthetic as an ideologically suspect and highly ambivalent project. Declaring an insurmountable gap between what the aesthetic wants and what it can realistically achieve, this now common critical position resigns itself to "clarifying the fundamental ambivalences and undecidabilities inherent in . . . [aesthetic] discourse," according to Pamela R. Matthew and David McWhirter.[3] As a consequence, the epochal wound that the aesthetic purports to mend is deemed unhealable, while the collective yearnings that still drive critics to theorize the aesthetic are left to reverberate without positive explanations, answers, or prospects.

As I have claimed throughout, the foregoing impasse stems from the modern era's disastrous dialectical opposition between money and aesthetics. Taking for granted the Liberal reduction of money to a private and alienable quantum of value, this dialectic pits aesthetic expansion against monetary contraction, sensuous diversity against abstract domination, and collective caretaking against reckless disintegration. Forever coming up against the inadequacies of both Liberal money and the aesthetic, this contest ensnares modern life in a series of seemingly intractable "ambivalences and undecidabilities" while unconsciously vitiating the redemptive capacities of each. The dialectic also forecloses money's public limitlessness, which, as I argued in chapter 1, Modern Monetary Theory reveals. It benumbs the sensorium to money's "proto-aesthetic" background, characterized in chapter 2 as the shared "sensory floor" conditioned by monetary governance as a whole. To recall the language of Thomism developed in chapter 3, the money/aesthetics dialectic banishes into illegibility the broad cascading mesh of mediation upon which all sensuous particulars rely.

Given the critical genealogy revealed in previous chapters, the time has come not only to negate and renounce the injurious modern dialectic between money and aesthetics but also to set this historical relationship upon positive and more salubrious bases. Here, then, I mean to recover the care that modernity's money/aesthetic dialectic has historically repressed, while restoring the curative capacities of each to its proper domain. In so doing, I charge critical aesthetics with a new mandate, namely, *to treat every historical artifact as a declaration of dependence and to understand all sensuous forms as cryptic indicators of the boundless public center toward which everything leans.* Guided by this mandate, aesthetic theory can develop social impulses within aesthetic artifacts that stand to enlarge and transform the money relation. Concurrently this critique must search aesthetic artifacts for symptoms of money's historical failures. In this way aesthetic critique will continue to express the social miseries unconsciously crystallized in social artifacts, fulfilling Adorno's well-known adage that "the need to lend a voice to suffering is a condition for all truth."[4] In the wake of MMT, however, critical theory must learn to see money's limitless center as the source of collective anguish. To redeem damaged life, critical theory must disclose money's untold capacities for cultivation and healing.

Florentine Gravity

There are not one but at least two gravities that shape Western modernity. The most legible and well-known form of gravity is, of course, the natural force of physical attraction described variously by Johannes Kepler, Galileo Galilei, and Isaac Newton.[5] We might name this force *gravitas rationalis*, designating its epistemological rationalism and grounding in mathematics as well as its ontological insistence upon harmony, balance, and proportion. In a very conscious and deliberate sense, gravitas rationalis filled the metaphysical vacuum left open after the collapse of scholastic theology. Denoting contiguous, observable, and ultimately calculable relations, gravitas rationalis replaced the transcendent causality and mediated co-presence known under Thomism with an allegedly naturalistic metaphysics rooted in haecceity and contiguous relations at a distance. For modern scientific rationality, gravitas rationalis meant iron-clad certitude. It also emerged, however, as a site of anxiety, ambivalence, and conflict. Skeptics such as philosopher Gottfried Wilhelm von Leibniz accused the likes of Newton of smuggling a "scholastic occult quality" into the science of gravity, allowing unnatural and noncontiguous action at a distance into a modern metaphysics that categorically did not permit it.[6] In turn, Immanuel Kant, Friedrich Schelling, and Friedrich Nietzsche lashed out against the mechanistic determinism of gravitas rationalis.[7] In opposition to gravity's all-determining horizon, these thinkers affirmed the exception of human freedom and the powers of organic nature to flout the commandments of modernity's mechanistic physics.

However, the modern epoch gives rise to another and wholly uncontested sense of gravity, which has hitherto received little critical attention. Crystallized in the visual culture of Renaissance Florence, this gravity owes to sense experience, feeling, and morality rather than scientific rationality. Unlike the gravity of modern science, it is contingent, affective, and mysterious. It unfolds as sensory impressions of a cosmic haecceity. To distinguish it from the dominant gravitas rationalis, I call this undertheorized Florentine gravity *gravitas passibilis*. From the Latin infinitive *pati, passibilis* designates a capacity for feeling, enduring, and, above all, suffering. It speaks, therefore, to the *passion* that motivates the gravitropic visuality of the Florentine Renaissance in contrast to the cold mechanics of gravitas rationalis that evolve in later modernity. Still, this contrast hardly constitutes an opposition. The gravitas passibilis of Florentine art not only predates the emergence of gravitas rationalis but also underwrites both the science of modern physics and its manifold rejections. It becomes modernity's basic mimetic comportment to the world. Thus, while gravitas rationalis composes contested theories of force and motion, gravitas passibilis constitutes a tacit mimetic comportment to the enigma of the whole.

The gravitropic visuality of Florence flourished in tandem with humanistic methods and pedagogy during the crucial passage of the Renaissance. As with gravitas rationalis, it sought to describe a world of bodies, forces, and motion. Art historian Michael Baxandall sees the relationship between Renaissance painting and writing as one of mutual influence.[8] Humanists such as Petrarch drew heavily on analogies between painting and writing, he explains.[9] Painters, architects, and sculptors transferred the humanistic principle of *compositio*—a coherent physical arrangement or sequence—from the realm of humanist writings to the visual sphere.[10] Distinguished by humanists from the degraded form of medieval *dissolutio*, *compositio* opposed the former's disintegrated and essentially paratactic floridness.[11] On Baxandall's reading, the *compositio/dissolutio* distinction informed both Florentine writing and painting, and it was Leon Battista Alberti who would explicitly close the loop between the two spheres. In publications such as *Della pittura* (1435) and *Della statua* (1450), Alberti set forth a theory of art criticism that overtly compared the *compositio* of humanistic writing to the visual *compositio* he uncovered in works by Giotto, Brunelleschi, Donatello, and Masaccio.[12]

Upon closer inspection, however, a division of emphasis and labor distinguishes the period's humanist and visual methods. Humanist writings tend to underscore spectacles of disintegration that threaten a world of contingent actions. Thus, while neoclassical *compositio* ruled the formal construction of humanist writing, its integrating form was regularly put in the service of scenes of material *dissolutio*. By contrast, Florentine visual culture of the Early and High Renaissance seems to have been more interested in securing spectators against the menace of *dissolutio*. It did so by joining form to content and enfolding viewers and figures alike in gravity's assuring omnipresence. Unlike Byzantine and Gothic abstraction, therefore, Florentine visuality engaged anxious spectators in an impassioned gravitropic drama, one that simultaneously contracted the topology of the sacred and furnished the senses with new agonies and joys.

FIG. 1. Masaccio, *The Holy Trinity, with the Virgin and Saint John and Donors*, 1425.

To discern this transformation in visual culture, it is crucial to understand art's allegorical function during the period. Forever allegorizing complex relations to the totality, art allegorizes the money medium that conditions it in particular. Frequently, the work is deliberate, yet intentions never wholly square with results. Instead, these results tend to be formally unstable and socially messy. When it comes to Florentine art and gravitropic visuality, we might point to Masaccio's 1425 fresco *The Holy Trinity, with the Virgin and Saint John and Donors* (fig. 1).

An altarpiece housed in the Dominican Church of Santa Maria Novella in Florence, the painting is an archetype of Quattrocento art and represents the earliest known example of mature one-point linear perspective. Roughly ten and half feet across and nearly twenty-two feet tall, Masaccio's fresco is hailed for its commanding physical presence, tactile corporeality, chiaroscuro modeling, foreshortened architectural elements, and overall compositional balance. Tracing a pyramid that slopes from top to bottom of the painting, *The Holy Trinity* features God supporting Jesus, who is suspended in the center of a high and deep vault. Between them, a dove representing the Holy Spirit descends from Father to Son. Mary and John stand on a high step that is more proximate to the viewer, flanking the Holy Trinity from above and both sides. Farther down and still nearer, the donors who commissioned the work kneel on a middle step. The pair stands more widely apart than Mary and John, expanding the pyramidal structure. From mysterious apex to mortal ground, therefore, the pyramid slopes down and toward spectators. Viewers, in return, look up to receive divine grace.

The bottom of the pyramid corresponds with the painting's ground level, giving its Trinitarian geometry a firm material foundation. Beneath the foundation, moreover, looms an underground crypt, supported, like the architecture above it, by physical columns. Pushed to the foreground of spectatorial space, this crypt houses a tomb with skeletal remains and an inscription that reads: "I once was what you are now; what I am you shall be." Marking this space as a *memento mori*, the sarcophagus and accompanying text are reminders of life's frailty and inevitable end. Yet this reminder's unequivocal materiality lends the scene a deeply phenomenological, rather than merely symbolic, significance. Indeed, its physicality not only exposes the painting's Trinitarian geometry to precarious earthly foundations but also exerts a pull on Masaccio's composition that renders everything erect and enduring in the painting all the more miraculous. In this way the work turns inexorable gravity into a meta-medium by which salvation becomes possible. Devotional practice becomes, by extension, a distinctly gravitropic passion.

In transforming gravity into this meta-medium, *The Holy Trinity* relies on a signifying instrument that nineteenth-century American pragmatist C. S. Peirce would term the *index*. As opposed to symbolic and iconic signs, which function according to conventionality and similitude, respectively, the index involves spatial immediacy and physical contiguity. "The index is physically connected with its object," Peirce writes; "they make an organic pair."[13] Additionally, the index constitutes what is called a "deictic" sign, which, while transferable across many contexts, denotes a specific happening within a circumscribed location and time. In this sense the index contracts worldly forces to a material point. At the same time, however, it physically points to the broad background that precipitated the occurrence. Footprints; photographs; weathervanes; a person's gait; medical symptoms; a pointing finger: such are the commonly cited examples of indexical signs. Curiously, many of these conjure a wedge-shaped intersection, or V-like pattern, to indicate focalization and convergence on one hand and broader dynamics on the other. If such figures recall haecceity, this is because indices are the semiotic face of haecceity's metaphysics of thisness. They are, in other words, its paramount signifying instrument.

On this view, the index was central to gravitropic visuality long before modern media theorists drew upon the sign to account for the contingencies of photography and cinema. No doubt, the phenomenal texture of Masaccio's painting derives, in part, from its abstract, totalizing, and allegedly "rational" geometry. Here, however, rational planning serves an immanent restlessness. Indexicality blisters beneath *The Holy Trinity*'s veneer of order, balance, and solemnity, granting a field composed of contiguous and contingent emanations. It expresses a foundational element of Florentine visual culture, which as with Masaccio's fresco, makes immanent visual experience the basis of pictorial value. The index thus offers the phenomenological crux of a novel faith in the indissoluble contiguity of the invisible. It establishes the needle's eye through which the crisscrossing threads of Florentine gravity must pass.

Fiscal Mimesis

The Holy Trinity blatantly dramatizes the anxious reversibility of its visual regime's gravitropic bond. In so doing it immerses viewers in a visual equivalent to the covenantal metaphysics developed in the writings of Franciscan theologians and Florentine humanists. As Ozment reminds us, the period's covenantal metaphysics held that "the world was contingent, not necessary and [that] only concepts, words, and promises bound man to God and to the world."[14] In *The Holy Trinity* it is gravitropism that tethers the sensorium to God and the world, as Masaccio's depiction of the Holy Spirit indicates. Represented as a flying dove, the Holy Spirit shares the index's characteristic V shape as it plunges downward from God, the father, to the cusp of Jesus's golden halo (fig. 2).

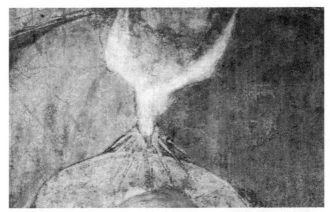

FIG. 2. The Holy Spirit as flying dove shooting toward Christ's golden halo. Detail, Masaccio, *The Holy Trinity, with the Virgin and Saint John and Donors*, 1425.

Its wedge-like depiction thus narrows the forces surrounding its winged body, concentrating them into the bird's sharp and compacted beak. This convergence shoots forth a divine radiance, which continues the spirit's gravitropic trajectory and distributes God's grace downward to Jesus and viewer alike. God, meanwhile, ensures His grace will arrive at its destination by manually supporting the crossbeam on which the Son's body is draped. In this sense God's support of the crucifix allegorizes the gravitropic covenant orchestrated by *The Holy Trinity* as a whole. As the kneeling faithful await divine gifts to trickle down from on high, the painting's form makes sure nothing in the picture escapes God's full and sweeping embrace.

And yet, *The Holy Trinity* also reveals the extent to which its aesthetic covenant structurally fails to provision everyone. Despite its supporting architecture, the work's gravitropic visuality remains a contingent configuration and, as Masaccio's *memento mori* suggests, its disintegration is inevitable. The painting's gravitropic phenomenology likewise presumes that grace must push through contiguous space from an invisible elsewhere before arriving at the perceptible here and now. Its divine gift is, therefore, forever on the brink of arrival, perpetually appearing and falling away. Alberti theorizes this brink in his conception of the containing edge, which strives to enclose and fill up embodied space through indexicality's immanent touch. A mobile boundary, the containing edge is haecceity's mark on the visible. Its perpetual binding of infinitude guarantees the inadequacy of Florentine gravity's universal covenant. Small wonder, then, that images of out-stretched arms and pointing fingers figure so prominently in Florentine painting. They distill the efforts of an immanent contour, at once creating and maintaining everything that is. Giotto's *Saint Francis Renounces His Father* (1297) depicts an intimate encounter wherein Francis reaches upward toward God's blessing hand, which itself pokes downward through an opening in the sky (fig. 3). More emblematic is Michelangelo's *Creation of Adam* (1508–12) on the ceiling of the Sistine Chapel (fig. 4). Here God's body stretches toward a languid and lifeless Adam, who lies waiting to receive the divine spark of life from God's extended finger.

The purpose of Renaissance painting, meanwhile, is estab-lished by the viewpoint of Quattrocento perspective, which not only composes the crux of Florentine gravity but also anchors its many indices. A heterogeneous assemblage, this viewpoint marks the convergence of one-, two-, even three-point linear systems. It is conjured through horizon lines, vanishing points, and foreshortening as well as through atmospheric effects such as overlapping, color desaturation, and contrast reduction. In all cases, perspective compresses the sensorium to a finite and more or less grounded look that encompasses yet exceeds the picture's own gaze. As a result, the gaze, like the look, is situated and limiting, proceeding from a finite indexical place in spite

FIG. 3. Francis reaches toward God's blessing hand in the sky. Giotto, *Saint Francis Renounces His Father*, 1297.

of its apparent grandeur. Still, it is the gaze and not the look that settles and determines the scene. Engendering stable distributions of proximity and distance, heaviness and lightness, density and diaphanousness, the gaze locates, holds, and weighs down the viewpoint, which, for all its intensity and locatedness, exerts comparatively little force on the scene.

And yet, look and gaze form an unstable covenant in Quattrocento perspective, forging a bond that, like the wax seal on a contract, eventually breaks or melts away. This bond's

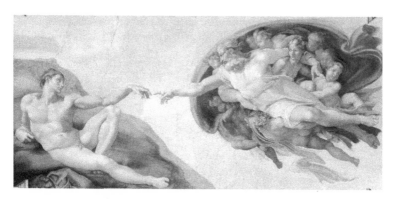

FIG. 4. Adam waits to receive the divine spark of life from God's extended finger. Michelangelo, *Creation of Adam*, 1508–12.

temporariness owes to perspective's allegiance to contiguous motion, movements that are, as Alberti writes, "made by changing place."[15] Indeed, because perspective restricts relationality to local interactions, it bars the assurances proffered by Thomist co-presence as well as the infinitude suggested by Byzantine and Gothic abstraction. Emerging from a play of mutually exclusive positions, perspectivalism supplants spatial coincidence with temporal succession and a boundless infinity with perpetual flux. The result opens a vacuum in visuality. Felt as indefinite postponement or inevitable loss, this vacuum appears in the guise of haecceity's self-containment while belying a fundamentally evacuative phenomenology that forecloses being at multiple locations. Thus, like a coin-starved purse, perspective precipitates two reciprocally undermining activities: contracting perception to a hemorrhaging haecceity, it widens perception to as much as haecceity allows. The risk lies in the compact between contraction and expansion, which, as with the look and the gaze, must stabilize an increasingly unstable sensorium.

This picture in mind, I propose a theory of mimetic likeness in Quattrocento perspective that departs from conventional accounts. Rather than presume nature as its gravitropic model, I offer the Florentine money form as perspective's primary mimetic object. To be sure, art historians have long linked perspective to the mathematically exacting money culture of Renaissance Florence, which discovered in nature its own fondness for measurement, calculation, and geometrical exactitude. Marxists, too, connect perspective to Florentine money, though they reject the abstract dominion they attribute to each. For both groups, perspective imitates an unquestionably private, finite, and alienable money relation. My view, by contrast, follows MMT's vision of money as a boundless public center. As such, perspective mirrors the convulsive Florentine fisc, which, I argued in chapter 3, the city-state straightjacketed when it won monetary independence during the War of the Eight Saints. "Acutely concerned about the fisc," according to historian Gene A. Brucker, the polity that gave rise to Brunelleschi, Donatello, and Masaccio expressed contradictory desires.[16] Longing to expand the public purse, it also contracted the city-state's expenditures. Quattrocento perspective mimes this contradiction, I argue, constructing a gravitropic phenomenology that overtakes the phenomenology of perception in general. More than humanist pedagogy, that is, which served literate elites, Florence's gravitropic visuality transformed the collective spaces all social classes inhabited. Above all, it transfigured the space of the Church, constricting the presumed transcendence of Gothic abstraction and Eucharistic mediation from the inside out.

The story of Florentine visuality, however, has been repressed from the start. Peterson notes how civic and religious projects from the early fifteenth century willfully repressed the history of the War of the Eight Saints, falsely blaming the Milanese so as to construct a positive image of the papacy and church. "If the memories . . . being inscribed into the city's sacred urban fabric were to be piously conveyed to posterity," then, writes Peterson, "the legitimizing narrative of the Florentine republic would have to be detached from much of the history of its own church."[17] What Peterson omits from this history is gravitropic perspective, which defined not only this aesthetic project but also its unwitting mimesis of Florence's crisis-ridden fisc. Involving citizens across multiple economic strata, gravitropic visuality transformed the interior surfaces of the church and civic institutions, where it did not repudiate Gothic abstraction and Eucharistic mediation so much as erode their claims on perception. Aligning perspective with the church's Gothic interior, Masaccio used aggressive *tromp-l'oeil* effects in *The Holy Trinity* to complement gravitropism's contraction of the sensorium as such.

Aesthetic Gravity

Over subsequent centuries the Florentine money form spread throughout Western Europe, and so, too, did its metaphysics of haecceity and gravitropic visuality. The principal movers behind the dissemination were Protestant reformers and Catholic counter-reformers, who variously appealed to intellectual systems grounded in haecceity to revolutionize Western political economy. Decentering good works from Church mediation, the Reformation anchored salvation in a precarious covenantal faith (*sola fides*) and an intimate and immediate relation with scripture (*sola scriptura*). The Counter-Reformation, by contrast, developed a more personal and direct Catholicism, incorporating laypersons in activities from which they were previously excluded. It was the Calvinists, however, who weaponized and internationalized haecceity, turning the domain of sensuous immediacy toward radical political and economic ends. Compounding the period's destruction of and divestment from Church property, Calvinism's political and economic pursuit of immediate association and divine assurance leveraged secular authorities against the Church's authority and wealth. The resulting expansion of confession was the occasion for the French Wars of Religion, the English Civil War, and the cataclysmic Thirty Years' War, all transacted in the name of the phenomenal immediacy that Franciscan theologians first articulated and Florentine humanists and painters developed.

Along the way, divergent visual cultures united in a common commitment to haecceity. Iconoclastic Calvinists whitewashed church walls to affirm the grounded immediacy of architecture against pictorial claims on transcendence. In the Protestant Netherlands, painters such as Rembrandt van Rijn (1606–69), Jacob van Ruisdael (1629–70), Johannes Vermeer (1632–75), and Pieter de Hooch (1629–84) developed a modest, delicate, and fleeting gravitropism, which was eagerly consumed by economically insecure members of the Dutch middle class. Elsewhere, artists such Peter Paul Rubens (1577–1640), Michelangelo da Caravaggio (1571–1610), Nicholas Poussin (1594–1665), and Gian Lorenzo Bernini (1598–1680) contorted, destabilized, and spectacularized Renaissance gravitropics for the Baroque tradition. Here classical proportion and balance, which had once comforted Renaissance viewers, yielded to insecure, harrowing, and impassioned scenes of falling, coming apart, and tarrying endlessly at the edge of obscurity and oblivion. As with Mannerism, Dutch painting, and even Calvinist whitewashing, Baroque works paradoxically turned sensations of loss, descent, and disintegration into assuring affections and rhythms.

Increasingly, then, the gravitropism of Renaissance Florence became the underlying *topos* of Liberal modernity, the Ur-image through which bourgeois elites envisioned and addressed the totality. In his unpublished *De Gravitatione*, for instance, Newton grounded universal gravity and absolute space in an impassioned theology. He called gravitational attraction "an emanative effect of God and an affection of every kind of being" and referred space to a decentered God's all-containing "sensorium."[18] A symptom of the Liberal money form, Newton's desire for God's decentered embrace grew, I argue, into the phenomenological basis of the modern aesthetic project. Rather than physical gravity, however, British and German philosophers appealed to a gravitas passibilis. In their writings the aesthetic offered a rich, expansive, and supportive gathering that linked bodily sensations to haecceity's suprasensible omnipresence. It thus served to redeem the habit of thisness to disintegrate in the domain of political economy.

Some thinkers, including the early Marx and late Heidegger, expressly thematize the kinship between aesthetics and gravity. Most philosophers obscure the relationship, however, by opposing the determinism of physics to aesthetic freedom.[19] Kant's seminal contribution to aesthetic philosophy is telling in this regard. As Michael Friedman has argued, Kant's critical refashioning of Newtonian physics in *Metaphysical Foundations of Natural Science* (1786) played an important role in shaping his mature philosophy. It is true that Kant's transcendental thinking eschewed the substantial ontology proffered by Newton's commitments to a divine sensorium and affective gravitation. Yet throughout his later writings, "Kant saw a deep analogy between the community of all rational beings in a moral realm of ends and the thoroughgoing community effected among all material bodies in the universe by universal gravitation."[20] Kant valued Newton's analogy between moral and physical gravity because it promised the harmony and order the philosopher craved. Still, Kant sidestepped Newton's theological physics, severing the link between moral and physical gravitation to formulate an immanent understanding of practical gravitation that one might call "gravitropic idealism." This idealism, which abandoned affective forces and an immaterial prime mover, nonetheless retained the ordering purposiveness around which Kant's critical metaphysics were built.

Indeed, Kant made his gravitropic idealism the implicit foundation of his critical philosophy, according to Friedman. "An injection of *our* pure intellect into *our* pure forms of sensibility . . . takes the place," writes Friedman, "of Kant's pre-critical doctrine that a schema of the divine intellect, by an analogue of Newtonian divine omnipresence, is ultimately responsible for the order we perceive in the physical world."[21] Kant's *Critique of Judgment* makes the most of this substitution of immanent for divine ordering, transforming the aesthetic into a site of modern salvation, characterizing it as a "physicoteleological" pursuit from which he hopes a new theology might develop. Of course, Kant's aesthetic philosophy cloaks its gravitropic structure by largely avoiding explicit references to gravitational attraction. As Friedman's analysis reveals, however, the aesthetic project Kant birthed nevertheless takes a decidedly gravitropic shape. Fashioning the aesthetic in the image of Newton's gravitas passibilis—itself a product of Florentine visual culture—Kant rejects scholastic theology and banishes immaterial causes and mediated co-presence from the field of aesthetic redemption.

This brings me to one of my book's key theses: *The aesthetic project constitutes a gravitropic form of care, but it is tragically incapable of fulfilling its historical charge.* Answering the apparent privation of money, the aesthetic fills up, expands, and secures a sensorium that money depletes, contracts, and dissolves. Its gravitropic impulse is, for this reason, doubly inadequate. First, in pitting aesthetics against the monetary relation, gravitropism suppresses the saving powers of money, asphyxiating it and aesthetics alike. Second, in seeking to redeem the haecceity of Liberal money, gravitropism hides the aesthetic project's mimesis of the monetary relation, including that relation's abstract collective care. Even aesthetic practices that embrace abstraction ultimately prove gravitropic. Situating the former inside the latter, they eradicate abstraction's mediating co-presence and render imperceptible the aesthetic's dependence on money's communal bounty.

The aesthetic signals thus the limit of modern care. Rejecting divine mediation at a distance, modernity adopts the aesthetic's gravitropic embrace, stretching haecceity to its maximal capacity in the hopes of redeeming the social totality. A vital and by now inextricable feature of modern life, the aesthetic contributes to political and economic domains. In making it a site of collective salvation, however, one turns from money's limitless center and obliges the aesthetic to contribute more than it can afford. Contemporary aestheticians know the hopelessness of this charge but do not perceive its conditions. Melancholically renouncing the dialectic between money and aesthetics, they fail to detect the debilitating history of this relation or to imagine a genuinely curative way forward.

To transcend this impasse, critique after MMT must realize sublation by other means. These means include an avowedly chartalist reconfiguration of aesthetics and collective life that not only folds the aesthetic into money's horizon of care but also turns critique toward the total sensory, or *proto-aesthetic*, field that money engenders. To transcend the money/aesthetics dialectic fully, however, theoreticians must discern and treat its entrenched symptomology, including their own affections for melting solids and gravitropic assurances. Critical theory cannot simply denounce or dismiss the spectacles of disintegration and compensatory gravitropics that drive the dialectic. Rather, it must approach gravitropic suffering and caretaking as declarations of dependence and impassioned demands for a more expansive, diverse, and secure collectivity, particularly in the face of neoliberalism's debilitating relationship to abstraction.

That *Never* Happens to Errol Flynn

To set out the problem of aesthetic abstraction in the neoliberal period, I want to consider a midcentury American artifact, which, like many of the era's cultural productions, offers a fairly blithe relationship to the subject. The artifact is the Daffy Duck short *The Scarlet Pumpernickel* (1950), a Chuck Jones *Merrie Melodies* send-up of the 1940s swashbuckler. Midway through the short Daffy leaps from a high castle window. Rather than mount the steed waiting patiently below, the duck splats headfirst onto the ground. With sword bent and stars whirling about his quashed Cavalier hat, Daffy addresses the cinematic audience directly: "That's funny," he says with his characteristic lisp, "that *never* happens to Errol Flynn."[22]

The joke, I reckon, is directed at two sources simultaneously: The most obvious, Errol Flynn action-adventure films; the other, Disney's Golden Age of animation. Though the former delight in graceful leaps and bounds, they never brandish their hero's unseen falls and impacts. Midcentury Disney features, meanwhile, were typically well staffed. They offered smooth and fully animated environments with relatively naturalistic movements. Warner Brothers' shorts, by contrast, were underfunded, understaffed, and thus obliged to use more staccato "limited animation" techniques. Such techniques reduced the amount of drawings required for a total work. However limited, Warner Brothers' cartoons turned their aesthetic toward thwarting, even mocking, the classicism of Disney. Against the latter's modest "squash and stretch" character animation and gentle gravitational physics, Warner Brothers reveled in abstract figurations that unpredictably alternated between violently exaggerated physical interactions and suspensions of gravitational physics altogether. Thus, while *The Scarlet Pumpernickel* explicitly targets Errol Flynn, Daffy might just as well have said, "That's funny, that *never* happens to Bambi."

Looking to *The Scarlet Pumpernickel* from a contemporary neoliberal context, we can see a third and unexpected reading of Daffy's jibe emerge. In this case, meaning derives from the joke's phenomenological *un*intelligibility. For a child today, Daffy's one-liner makes little sense, not simply because Errol Flynn and studio rivalries are unknown but also because the dominant phenomenology of screen movement has been thoroughly reorganized. Since the inception of the New Hollywood blockbuster alongside neoliberalism in the late 1970s, nearly all action figures have come to tumble, collide, smash, and grind their way through screen space. From the vantage of franchises such as *Star Wars* (1977–present), *Toy Story* (1995–present), and *Quake* (1996–present), Daffy's emphatic crash is hardly aberrant. Such things *always* befall today's falling Errol Flynns. For this reason, I contend, *The Scarlet Pumpernickel* offers an uncanny proleptic significance. Intelligible only in retrospect, the cartoon puts into relief what distinguishes midcentury from post-'70s screen action. It also points to the distinct *phenomenologies of abstraction* that shape the periods as wholes.

Coming after aesthetic experiments in modernist abstraction, midcentury cultural production embraced formal and technological abstraction as *the* semiology of white middle-class uplift. In cinema as well as the industrial, popular, and fine arts, abstraction's defamiliarization of local coordinates and suspension of gravitropic logics embodied a fiscally robust postwar political economy defined by hubris, dynamism, and ease. The era was tarnished, of course, by sexism, racism, and homophobia as well as communist paranoia, nuclear threat, and environmental degradation. Yet the fact that this was no Shangri-La was hardly news, even for the culture industry itself. In Hitchcock's *Vertigo* (1958), confident Midge pokes fun at the patriarchal bases of both monetary and aesthetic abstraction. A middle-class commercial artist, Midge works from a studio apartment adorned with modernist paintings. Referring to a new-fangled brassiere designed on the model of a cantilever bridge, Midge waxes wryly on the "revolutionary uplift" such innovations allegedly provide. Hardly radical, midcentury America is riddled with inequalities and contradictions.[23] Nonetheless the era's fiscal expansion is historically unprecedented and its celebration of all things abstract a mimetic extension of this expansion.

Viewed this way, midcentury modernism departs from conventional accounts. Though it generalized, commercialized, and, in the judgment of many, degraded modernist and avant-gardist abstraction, midcentury modernism also inverted abstraction's expressed social significance. An exit from the world for many early twentieth-century artists, abstraction promised a utopian overcoming of bourgeois alienation and socioeconomic misery. "The more horrifying this world becomes," writes Bauhaus artist Paul Klee (1879–1940), "the more art becomes abstract. . . . [A] world at peace," he continues, "produces realistic art."[24] Under midcentury modernism, by contrast, abstraction realized—that is, made perceptible and socially palpable—a new political and economic order characterized by unprecedented prosperity, innovation, and security.

Of course, midcentury America never pushed outside or beyond the Liberal money form. An international Gold Standard and perpetual handwringing over federal deficits were key features of the era. Still, the period was defined by an enormous public sector: enlarged social safety nets; legal protections for unions; firewalls between commercial banking and financial investing; and countercyclical spending that kept aggregate demand relatively high and stable. The era's oft-noted "optimism" owes in part to these transformations in the money relation. It owes equally to midcentury modernism's variously spacious, sleek, synthetic, colorful, invigorating, and avowedly abstract aesthetics. Such forms include sans serif typography, post-and-beam architecture, and the upward-sloping roofs and starbursts of the Atomic Age and Space Age. They encompass tapered-leg furniture, Hi-Fi, and plastic, as well as cocktail dresses, Martini glasses, and the suspension of foodstuffs in gelatin. Abstraction was not, in other words, merely white middle-class uplift. It was a phenomenal leap into a kind of collective floating.

From this perspective, Warner Brothers and Disney cartoons seem more like two species of the same historical genus. That genus is the Classical Hollywood Cinema and its noted continuity aesthetics. Identified by their relatively homogenous and linear constructions of space and time, these aesthetics were also known for their gloss, glamour, and dreamlike qualities. Technicolor, mobile cameras, and seamless editing: these supplied a phenomenology that film theorist Christian Metz once described as a "diffuse, geographically undifferentiated . . . *hovering*."[25] Meanwhile, with its regular use of rear and front projection, especially in driving scenes, classical Hollywood created ambiguous disjunctions between foreground and background, asserting the synthetic and abstract nature of screen movement, which animation likewise flaunted. In their book *Design in Motion* (1962), John Halas and Roger Manvell hailed animation as a key contributor to the era's love affair with abstraction.

> Abstract art takes purely formal values, some of which are present in the roots of nature, and makes these values the basis of art. . . . Animation extends this intellectual concept of visual beauty by adding mobility to its form. It enables abstract art to exist in time as well as space.[26]

Here abstraction composes an "intellectual" form with only tenuous roots in nature. Animation, by extension, is abstraction made mobile and temporal. Animation obeys unique non-topographical laws, not natural laws of motion and gravity.

Implying neither weight nor texture, according to Halas and Manvell, animation is irreducible to volumetric rises and falls in proximally differentiated space.

Midcentury Warner Brothers' cartoons turned nontopographical abstractions against Hollywood continuity aesthetics. In doing so, however, animators went furthest in revealing what might be called the budding neo-Thomist phenomenology of midcentury animation, Classical Hollywood cinema, and midcentury modernism writ large. Warner cartoons express an untroubled trust in abstraction, unfolding in a total sensory field. Within this field, matter and its sundry local motions are conditioned and supported by a centralized source of meaning. Variously employing hyperbolic physics, nontopographical movements, material gatherings, and apparent dissolutions, the contiguous relations in these cartoons do not immanently determine meaning at the site of their contours. Rather, animated movements realize a cascade of matter and meaning that endures continuously regardless of form's individual fluctuations.

A vivid example of the neo-Thomist impulses in Warner animation can be found in another Chuck Jones send-up: *Duck Dodgers in the 24½th Century* (1953). A friendly parody of earlier sci-fi B pictures such as *Buck Rodgers* (1939), *Duck Dodgers* wreaks havoc on midcentury's abstract and hypertechnical Space Age aesthetics while critiquing the environmental extractions and catastrophic geopolitics that drove the Cold War. At the outset a virtual camera cranes quickly upward, following a yellow taxi through a seemingly groundless space city. Its architecture suggests the period's so-called "Googie" style with characteristic diagonals, parabolas, soft parallelograms, atomic shapes, bulbous antennae, and myriad grids of glass. Once inside, Daffy Duck sketches bewilderingly convoluted travel plans to Planet X (fig. 5).

His mission: to claim it and its deposits of Alludium Phosdex—the "shaving cream atom"—for Earth. Contested

FIG. 5. Daffy Duck as Duck Dodgers sketches a dizzyingly abstract route to Planet X. Chuck Jones, *Duck Dodgers in the 24½th Century*, 1953.

by Marvin the Martian, Daffy proclaims, "There just ain't room enough on this planet for the two of us!"[27] In response Marvin takes aim at the duck with his "Acme A-1 Disintegrating Pistol." Assuring the audience his "Disintegration Proof Vest" will protect him, Daffy is blasted to smithereens, leaving his vest momentarily suspended in midair.[28] He is immediately reconstituted by his sidekick's "Acme Integrating Pistol." With this, the film nods to the laws that underwrite every Warner Brothers cartoon. Namely, a boundless center of abstraction conditions all matter and meaning, and no matter how contingent or disintegrative, local comings and goings are incapable of ever overturning the whole's metaphysics.

Despite the contrast attributed to Warner Brothers and Golden Age Disney animation, I argue that Disney, too, embodies neo-Thomist impulses. For all its classicism, naturalism, and seeming devotion to gravity, midcentury Disney uses abstraction to create an effervescent and malleable gravitropics that belie their midcentury foundations. Disney features from *Fantasia* (1940) and *Dumbo* (1941) to *Alice in Wonderland* (1951) include hallucination and dream sequences that forestall and circumvent gravitropic logics. In *Cinderella* (1948) a hot drop of tea is miraculously sucked back into the pot from which it dangles, and *Peter Pan* (1953) regularly flouts gravitational physics in scenes that rival Warner Brothers' creations. Even into the 1960s Disney pushed abstraction. Googie aesthetics met abstract relativity in the *Man in Space* (1955) series, while *101 Dalmatians* (1962) featured Xerox copy scan lines that gave it the look and feel of an animated sketchbook.

Over the course of the 1960s Kennedy liberalism and Goldwater conservatism gave way on one hand to antiwar protests, the counterculture, and Black Power, and on the other to the Wallace backlash and Nixon's "silent majority." Though midcentury abstraction continued to inform fashion, advertising, and the space race above all, aesthetic production increasingly rejected modern sleekness and white patriarchal managerialism. Thus, aesthetically and sociopolitically, the late 1960s and early 1970s were periods of experimentation, contestation, and flux: Pop Art, Fluxus, flower power, and psychedelia; Black is Beautiful, *Sesame Street*, buckskins, and beards. The era saw competing color palettes from Day-Glo fluorescents to muted earth tones. "This turbulent decade is hard to pin down," reads a present-day Pantone Company retrospective. "Was it idealistic or rebellious? Shaggy or stylish? Coarse or composed?"[29] If anything united these aesthetics, it was their dizzying reorganization of meaning and matter, which expressed a desire for the fresh and more diverse experiences the period often framed through rhetorics of "authenticity."

As film scholar Amy Rust has argued, postclassical cinema played a central role in shaping fantasies of authenticity during the late 1960s and early 1970s. With the financial collapse of the studio system and the Production Code's eradication, so-called Hollywood Renaissance directors, including Arthur Penn, Sam Peckinpah, Robert Altman, Martin Scorsese, and Francis Ford Coppola, not only brought more sex and violence to American screens but also broke up the old Hollywood continuity system. Influenced by the ambiguous forms of European art films and the located immediacies of Direct Cinema documentaries, these filmmakers pursued more authentic realities by returning historically repressed forms of abstraction and documentation to conventional genre pictures. Interested in depictions of violence, Rust in her analysis treats technologies such as multiple-camera montage, squibs with artificial blood, freeze-frames, and zooms as "figures" that, "part practice (*techne*), part discourse (*logos*), . . . join sensuous sights to sites of significance for an era self-consciously and, by many accounts, perilously preoccupied with violence."[30] Uniting "abstraction and concreteness, excess and control," these figures variously corroborate and challenge the period's faith in authentic disclosure, which was, Rust concludes, problematically classed, gendered, and racialized.[31]

Like many scholars and critics, Rust uncovers aesthetic and social potential in Hollywood Renaissance aesthetics. What interests me, however, is the blockbuster's subsequent squelching of this potential during "New Hollywood's" emergence in the late 1970s. Indeed, whereas the Hollywood Renaissance forged complex and open encounters with the abstract, New Hollywood's action-adventure mode established a debilitating relationship to abstraction that came to color the neoliberal period as a whole.

There, There

The New Hollywood blockbuster emerged amid oil shocks, unemployment, "stagflation," and increased financial leveraging. A broad-scale shift from American-style Keynesianism to

Chicago School monetarism, Hayekian free markets, and fiscal austerity marked its political moment.[32] A time of communal dis-aggregation, according to historian Bruce Schulman, a "process of fragmentation and separation" distinguished the period with "people discovering and cultivating distinct identities, going off by themselves, literally or figuratively."[33] It is important to remember, however, that the blockbuster followed America's last push of labor against capital. It also coincided with growing feminist and queer activism and the last great cross-coalition fight for a federal job guarantee.[34]

Pioneered by directors Steven Spielberg and George Lucas, as well as special effects artists such as Douglas Trumbull and Lucas's team at Industrial Light and Magic, the New Hollywood blockbuster combined postclassical aesthetics with B film genres such as science fiction, horror, and the western. Anchoring this combination in effects-driven action-adventure sequences, these filmmakers broke with the established history of Hollywood movement. Prefigured by *Jaws* (Spielberg, 1975) and inaugurated by *Close Encounters of the Third Kind* (Spielberg, 1977) and *Star Wars* (Lucas, 1977), the blockbuster replaced the flickering and often ambiguous ephemerality of Hollywood's "dream factory" with "rollercoaster" or "thrill ride" aesthetics. More important, it contracted the experience of screen movement to an immersive kinematics—a hyper-Newtonian phenomenology, as I have called it—that revived Florentine gravitropics to answer the perils of a bourgeoning neoliberal order.[35]

Key to New Hollywood physics, according to film scholar Julie Turnock, was the blockbuster's shift from "process photography" to "optical animation."[36] The dominant form of effects during the classical period, process photography was produced on set. It relied on conspicuous uses of front and rear projection that often led to ambiguous spatiotemporal constructions. Turning to optical animation, the blockbuster displaced effects work to postproduction, where motion control cameras and optical printers regulated the immersive, volumetric, and kinematic environments Turnock calls "integral continuous space."[37] The "special effects-driven blockbuster's aesthetic," she notes, is "overflowing with kinetic action, taking place within minutely detailed, intricately composited mise-en-scène, comprising an all-encompassing, expandable environment."[38] Thus, while the New Hollywood blockbuster may appear similar to earlier action-adventure or disaster films, the hyper-Newtonian phenomenology made possible by its distinctly immersive optical animation represents a clear break from the screen action of the past.

Equally important to this phenomenology are its densely textured, localized, and bass-laden soundtracks, crafted by sound engineers such as Ben Burtt and delivered by Dolby Surround Sound. Fast paced, dizzying, and perpetually testing the limits of continuity, blockbuster action-adventure sequences continued the Hollywood Renaissance tendency to break up the homogenous space-time of classical cinema. Unlike their predecessors, however, blockbusters carefully grounded visual fractures in punctuated yet enveloping soundscapes. Cradling and enlarging their frenetic optics, these deep and rich soundtracks fleshed out the blockbuster's "all-encompassing and expandable environment" from the inside. The result transfigured continuity aesthetics for a reborn, lucrative, and enormously popular post-1970s Hollywood cinema. Departing from classical Hollywood's hovering, synthetic, and continuous space-time, the hyper-Newtonian blockbuster transformed a visually perceptible continuity into a sound-driven and enduring contiguity. With an invisible mesh of clangs, crashes, and whooshes, this contiguity supports and extends New Hollywood's disorienting kinematics through routine rumbles and impacts.

Like most art, meanwhile, the blockbuster allegorizes its own operations. In *Star Wars*, Obi-Wan Kenobi's theological meditations on "the Force" offer audiences important lessons about the blockbuster's audiovisual regime. Obi-Wan instructs action-hungry Luke Skywalker to "feel the Force flowing through [him]" and to "stretch out with [his] feelings."[39] Later he promises that the Force's ubiquitous energy will maintain Luke in perpetuity. "The Force will be with you, *always*," the elder Jedi assures him, though Lucas surely knew—like the skeptical Han Solo—a post-Watergate audience might not go in for Obi-Wan's "hokey religion."[40] All the same, Lucas channels the gospel of the hyper-Newtonian blockbuster into Obi-Wan's sermonizing, as did Spielberg's *Close Encounters* with its sardonic protagonist, Roy Neary. In this, Lucas and Spielberg made faith a preoccupation of blockbuster narratives, encompassing franchises from *Indiana Jones* (1981–present) to *The Matrix* (1999–2003) to *Harry Potter* (2001–11).

Still, it hardly matters whether one accepts the blockbuster's theology or regards it as "simple tricks and nonsense," since the faith of the blockbuster is ever a function of its hyper-Newtonian phenomenology. Here, seeing alone is not the same as believing because faith requires bodily absorption and material engulfment in a frequently obstructed visual "close encounter." The original 1977 poster for *Close Encounters* enumerates as much: "Close Encounter of the First Kind: Sighting of a UFO; Close Encounter of the Second Kind: Physical Evidence; Close Encounter of the Third Kind: Contact." Since the release of *Close Encounters* and *Star Wars*, the blockbuster's faith in its hyper-Newtonian phenomenology has witnessed explosive growth, from the turn to digital Visual Effects (VFX), to Pixar-style animation, to physics-driven Triple-A video games. Whether one "believes" in neoliberal action media is by now a moot point. The enduring fact of hyper-Newtonian phenomenology proves one's faith, thereby redeeming Obi-Wan's original promise that the Force will always be with us.

A vehement return of gravitas passibilis, hyper-Newtonian action media mark the revenge of Renaissance gravitropics on the neoliberal period. More specifically, they set into motion the intensities, torsions, and sublime disintegrations that defined Baroque and other seventeenth-century art. Like Baroque visuality does, neoliberal action media triangulate aesthetic experience with an intimate indexicality and all-encompassing gravity. They also transmute sensations of loss, falling, and disintegration into assuring affections and rhythms. Miming a convulsive and dangerously misallocated fiscal apparatus, these affections and rhythms repeatedly register the feeling that "there's no there, there" under neoliberalism, as Gertrude Stein once said of Oakland. At the same time, an ardent "there, there" answers money's evacuation from neoliberal existence. Hyper-Newtonian action media are iterative, buoying, and endlessly diversifying. Yet in the process blockbusters exclude abstraction's boundless co-presence, even as they furnish nervous sensoria with disastrously insufficient forms of collective care.

Far from negating abstraction, however, post-1970s cinema forges an ambivalent and extraordinarily contradictory relationship to its mysterious mediations. Whereas action-adventure media fetishize abstraction through diegetic equipment and extradiegetic technophilia concerning their visual effects, they demonize, diminish, and repurpose abstraction toward hyper-Newtonian ends. In general, these media set formal and technological abstraction *atop* what Lucas and Spielberg insisted were "grounded," though disintegrating, worlds.[41] Though often strewn with abstract graphics and hi-tech equipment, post-1970s blockbusters reduce abstraction to the haecceity of an unsurpassable physics. They work to contain, if not utterly eliminate, abstraction's enigmatic arrangements of matter and meaning as well as near and far. Like before, this reduction is frequently allegorized within the media's own narratives, as when characters seek to align abstract information, maps, and visual displays with circumscribed locales, traces, and targets.

In fact, two procedures define the blockbuster's relation to midcentury abstraction, each negating *and* recuperating it, though in divergent manners. The first aligns midcentury abstraction with political malevolence and social alienation, from which it saves characters associated with the aesthetic. Consider, for instance, the sleek, cold blackness of Darth Vader; Spielberg's mindless technocrats; the computerized surveillance in *Terminator* (1984–2015) and *Diehard* (1988–present); and the sick homogeneity and conformity of life in *Fight Club* (1999) and *The Matrix* films. In each case, rough-and-tumble action destroys the tacit eroticism of midcentury abstraction at the same time as these hyper-Newtonian physics sublimely release characters from apparent evils. The second procedure works through nostalgia. Rather than demonize or negate the past, the neoliberal blockbuster longs to return to midcentury abstraction's structures of feeling. *Back to the Future* (1985–88) and *Toy Story* supply salient examples, though there are small touches too, such as the Marvin the Martian figurine in *Gravity* (Alfonso Cuarón, 2015).

For Lucas and Spielberg, midcentury nostalgia permeates their earliest efforts. Most demonstrable in efforts to lend mass, movement, and gravity to their favorite childhood serials, the pair also pine for lost abstractions in subtle and complex ways. In a scene from *Close Encounters*, scruffy-faced Roy awakens to suburban doldrums. In the foreground one spies the enormous mountain of mud that, according to Roy, "is important. [It] means something."[42] Above and behind him, space maps adorn walls, as does a speculative Space Age illustration straight from the 1950s. Off screen, one hears a television; it is airing *Duck Dodgers*. "All this stuff is coming down," Roy pronounces, pulling at the mound which, as he struggles, snaps off at its peak.[43]

Thrown back with a chunk of the mountain in his hand, Roy stares, dumbstruck awe overtaking his face. Approaching the camera, he comes into close up and offers an early illustration of what film critic Kevin B. Lee calls the "Spielberg Face." "If there is one recurring image," explains Lee,

> that defines the cinema of Steven Spielberg it is The Spielberg Face. Eyes open, staring in wordless wonder, in a moment when time stands still; but above all, a childlike surrender in the act of watching, both theirs and ours. It's as if their total submission to what they are seeing mirrors our own. The face tells us that a monumental event has happened. In doing so, it also tells us how we should feel.[44]

For Lee the Spielberg Face is an affective relay mechanism. It constitutes the mimetic core of Spielberg's cinema and has become a standard trope for injecting sublimity into most visual effects blockbusters. What Lee neglects, however, is what Roy displays: a desire for thisness, a longing for haecceity. Stepping forward, Roy sharpens our view of his visage. In the reverse shot, an eyeline match pushes in to the object of Roy's and our fascination: a model-sized version of Devil's Tower, the flat-topped mountain at which the film stages its conclusion. From shot to reverse shot, from stepping to pushing forward, Roy, spectator, and world are pressed closely together, while this spatial compression points toward an unknown temporal beyond.

Curious, in this regard, are the elements that accompany this disclosure. At the right of the frame, a yellow magazine page reads "GRAVITY" in all caps (fig. 6).

As if this were too subtle for Spielberg's design, the soundtrack rings with hyperbolic explosions that accompany the destruction of Planet X at the close of *Duck Dodgers*. Drawing past to present and substance to sign, *Close Encounters* aims to

FIG. 6. Point of view shot revealing a model of Devil's Tower and a magazine featuring the word *GRAVITY* in all caps. Steven Spielberg, *Close Encounters of the Third Kind*, 1977.

redeem midcentury abstraction through a sublime haecceity that promises contacts of cosmic proportions. When, therefore, Spielberg combines "GRAVITY" with an abstract Space Age cartoon, he not only recuperates the affect of midcentury modernism but also heralds the birth of screen movement's hyper-Newtonian phenomenology. Ambivalently containing and repurposing abstraction for an emergent neoliberal order, this phenomenology pivots on a fugitive thisness while striving for gravitropic deliverance.

Are You Satisfied with Your Care?

One of the few modes of entertainment with widespread appeal, hyper-Newtonian media maintain the collective sensorium in ways that obstruct abstraction's social capacities. In this sense the phenomenology of the blockbuster extends to the phenomenology of globalization in general. Accordingly, money belongs not to a governing center but to a transnational field of private fluctuations. Cash-poor polities compete for "global capital" to spur production and claim sorely needed tax revenues. Money hemorrhages, meanwhile, from everyone's coffers, save for the filthy rich. For this reason, neoliberal media follow the lead of Elon Musk, whose private aerospace firm suggests that gravity alone keeps money on earth. With their faith in haecceity, hyper-Newtonian productions promise preverbal, even precognitive, encounters that make dependents of us all. Holding globalization together, they ensure that no alternative phenomenologies of abstraction emerge.

In fact, the ambivalence toward abstraction that defines hyper-Newtonian media grows more acute under neoliberalism, imperiling society as a whole. Displacing abstraction from state-supported Keynesianism, the neoliberal age binds it to fiscal austerity, privatized culture, and precarious financial leveraging. Together, Wall Street and Silicon Valley make abstractions of data, design, and display into so many decentered relations. They forge a permanent state of uncertainty and suffering that ensures the social benefits of abstraction are enjoyed by fewer and fewer persons. Indeed, under this order, abstraction becomes a site of constant anxiety and an elusive object of collective desire. Conceived as material propinquity, it promises to repair the failures of neoliberalism by coinciding with its own forms of enjoyment and care. To wit, Wall Street and Silicon Valley drive and often directly finance the hyper-Newtonian media that keep globalization's phenomenology intact. Impoverishing abstraction, they also manage its fallout, directing social production toward films and games assuring viewers that there is a there, there.

Of course, there is no there, there, and gravitropic media offer cold comfort for those beset by poverty, sickness, and un- or underemployment. If there *is* anything in this world, meanwhile, it is an abstract, boundless, and centralized money relation that can be made to care for every person and environment. Yet hyper-Newtonian media express a potent historical

FIG. 7. Hiro and Baymax reach toward one another in a gesture of reciprocal care. Don Hall and Chris Williams, *Big Hero 6*, 2014.

contradiction: they announce the exhaustion of the dialectic between money and aesthetics, even as they compose the greatest obstacle to transcending it. Stoking desires for haecceity, post-1970s action-adventure media ensure the persistence of the Liberal money form. They continuously enact neoliberalism's imagined implosion of abstraction and propinquity. They double down on modernity's gravitropic salvation. And in ritually making gravitropic salvation into a commercial spectacle, they trumpet the end of the dialectic between money and aesthetics, while offering nothing else in its place. In another sense, however, the compulsive repetition of these film and games are themselves throbbing historical symptoms. Flaunting their gravitropic longings, neoliberal media beseech an expansive and all-enveloping field of force that declares the collective's dependence on their care. As such, these media expose the poverty of the money/aesthetics dialectic and the historical failure of its fantasmatic gravitas passiblis.

In this context, Disney's computer-animated feature *Big Hero 6* (2014) poses a question at the heart of neoliberal media and the aesthetic project as such. Each time its inflatable healthcare

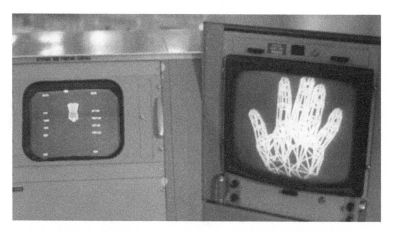

FIG. 8. Ed Catmull, "Computer Animated Hand," in Richard T. Heffron, *Future World*, 1976.

robot, Baymax, performs treatment, he asks: "Are you satisfied with your care?"[45] According to his programming, only a "yes" will suffice. For a media form that doles out lessons to its consumers, this affirmation seems cunningly reflexive and ideologically pernicious. Throughout *Big Hero 6*, Baymax's programming is played for humor. At the film's climax, his query becomes the source of a fatal and seemingly impossible decision. Free-floating in an alternative dimension of ponderous volumetric space, Baymax is damaged and can no longer use the majority of his powers. Thus stranded, he and protagonist Hiro reach out to stabilize each other's movements (fig. 7). Conjuring countless similar arrangements in hyper-Newtonian media, their interlocked grip recalls the computer-generated hand created by Pixar founder and president of Walt Disney Studios, Ed Catmull, in 1972 (fig. 8). A wire-form construction featured in the film *Futureworld* (1976), Catmull's hand pioneered the polygon projection techniques that have grounded more than four decades of gravitropic computer graphics.

FIG. 9. Hiro discovers Baymax's data chip in the latter's fist. Don Hall and Chris Williams, *Big Hero 6*, 2014.

Hiro and Baymax also return us to early modernity's gravitropic visuality. Recalling the figure of Francis reaching toward God's hand in *Saint Francis Renounces His Father* (fig. 3), the pair evoke above all Michelangelo's *Creation of Adam*, wherein God's outstretched finger expresses the contiguous and contingent foundations of human life (fig. 4). As they drift together and without recourse, Baymax offers to use his fist, an operational rocket, to propel Hiro back to safety. Because every action has its reaction, however, this means Baymax will be pushed deeper into the ether, where he will perish alone. Committed to this strategy, Baymax must nonetheless ask his routine question and receive an affirmative answer. When he asks Hiro, "Are you satisfied with your care?," the boy struggles to discover a way to save them both.[46] "There is no time," Baymax retorts before reiterating his question.[47] Rebuffed again, Baymax summons the origins of the blockbuster by way of Obi-Wan Kenobi. "Hiro," he pledges, "I will always be with you," to which the boy replies after another embrace: "I'm satisfied with my care."[48] Riding Baymax's fist to safety, Hiro's caretaker drifts toward the image's vanishing point.

Are we satisfied with our care: yes or no? Such is the choice we face when it comes to the fate of the modern dialectic between money and aesthetics. The conclusion to *Big Hero 6* offers the neoliberal path forward. Baymax returns to Hiro in the form of a data chip, clenched in the fist he rode to safety (fig. 9). A token of haecceity, the chip is a compact vehicle for storing abstract information that attains its place and significance against a gravitropic background. Delimited in space and contingent with respect to time, the chip permits Hiro to give back to Baymax and thereby helps him keep his caregiver's promise. As with the whole modern aesthetic project, *Big Hero 6* answers neoliberalism's zero-sum logic with a caring and mutually reciprocating haecceity. From MMT's vantage, of course, this contracted caretaking takes the very form of neoliberalism and, as such, represents a historical dead end. To retain the force of the aesthetic for our collective existence, we must refuse neoliberalism's false choice and enfold both money *and* aesthetics into abstraction's boundless and inalienable embrace. We must march, vote, write, and ultimately overtake the public monetary instrument that is ours. We must also learn, however, to give up the pleasures of gravitropic deliverance and embrace the shared difficulties of a boundless abstraction from monetary to aesthetic domains.

Epilogue

Becoming Second Nature

*Although in a way, it is possible for a glorified body to
be in the same place with another body: nevertheless,
the glorified body has the power within it to resist at
will anyone touching it, and thus it is palpable.*
—Thomas Aquinas

For me, abstraction is real, probably more real than nature.
—Joseph Albers

Critical theory remains an urgent undertaking, particularly as
neoliberalism's calamities deepen and nationalist demagogu-
ery threatens possibilities for pluralist democracy. Contrary to
what Max Horkheimer deemed "traditional theory," critical
theory affirms the historical character of social reality as well
as of sensory and conceptual organs by which this reality is
known. While traditional theory accommodates knowing to
being, moreover, critical theory abides the contradictions and
repressions, pains and injustices, that bind being and knowing
in a particular historical assemblage. Finally, if traditional theory merely describes reality in an effort to improve the extant,
critical theory aims to answer unheard suffering and cultivate
counter-hegemonic impulses so as to make a superior social

reality imaginable. Child- and eldercare crises, profit-driven incarceration, and climate change: such calamities are not rectified by neoliberal best practices and technological innovations. Totalizing in breadth, they tether interdependent needs and desires to multiple forms of production and distribution. What we require is a practice of critique that discloses neoliberalism's entangled sinews and, through this process, actualizes systemic and sustainable alternatives.

Yet to overcome neoliberalism, critical theory needs to abandon the impoverished Liberal ontology of money. A private, finite, and alienable quantum of value, Liberal money links private agents while evacuating and filling up decentralized space. Upheld by Marxists, though they critique its effects, this ontology finds fresh resistance when critical theory considers Modern Monetary Theory's bountiful conception of money. A political relationship between centralized governments and people, money, according to MMT, is an inalienable utility ever capable of expansion and reconstruction. Money obliges the public to a political center, socializing productive and distributive processes rather than organizing them locally and privately. As an abstract relation, moreover, money operates ubiquitously, simultaneously, and at a distance. Currency-issuing governments may be limited by real resources and ecological constraints, but money remains a resolutely infinite instrument. It is, at bottom, a function of legal inscription and political will, not immediate physics. Governments do not tax or borrow before spending. Indeed, because its capacities are limitless, money is forever capable of serving persons and environments. Neither international interdependency nor neoimperialist destruction can dispossess its powers of mediation.

The charge of critical theory, therefore, is to render perceptible money's boundless public center. Only then can it usher a more inclusive and less damaging world into being.

This is, of course, no small task. It is one thing to prove governments can afford to provide for all. It is quite another to confront how money perpetually shapes the social totality, including how its political withdrawal from some shapes social relations as a whole. This is because Liberal modernity has foreclosed the metaphysical scaffolding we need to perceive MMT's social topology. This includes images and words. We possess neither a grammar nor a poetics to make money's center palpable. Critical theory must, for this reason, invent new forms as well as recover ways of seeing and thinking from heterogeneous pasts.

Declarations of Dependence represents an unprecedented step in this direction. MMT's intervention, I have suggested, permits critical theory to transcend the dead-end dialectic between money and aesthetics. In chapter 1, I distinguish MMT's neo-chartalist theory of money from the exchange theory of the Liberal economic orthodoxy. Revealing money as boundless public utility organized by a centralized government, I claim money's capacious center as the source of political redemption in modernity. From there, I underscore the inadequacy of Liberal modernity's money/aesthetics dialectic, redressing social and ecological ills while simultaneously renewing the promise of the aesthetic by folding it into money's greater capacity for redemption. In chapter 2 I argue that money composes the center of collective caretaking in modernity. More important, it articulates a politics of care grounded in humanity's unavoidable social dependency. Drawing on Butler's work as well as the object-relations school of psychoanalysis, I develop a symptomology of care that understands the symptom as deriving not merely from repression but also from problems immanent to collective maintenance. Along the way, I theorize what I call money's proto-aesthetic field, defined as the shared sensory floor that monetary governance engenders.

Turning from the neoliberal present to modernity's past, chapter 3 proffers a new account of money's ascent in the modern age. Rethinking the Liberal metaphysics that have so hindered collective life, I uncover a more capacious conception of mediation in Thomas Aquinas's synthesis of late medieval scholasticism. Coincident with the expanding political economy of the High Middle Ages, Thomism envisioned mediation as a centralized cascade that realized God's infinite potential at simultaneous distances. Thomism also underwrote a legal articulation of the holy fisc, characterized in this case as an abstract, inalienable, and ubiquitous public purse. As I explain, however, political and ecological crises precipitated a contraction in Western metaphysics. Robbing Thomism of its centralized ontological supports, Franciscan nominalists and Florentine humanists variously bound mediation to a decentered haecceity that was perpetually haunted by spectacles of disintegration. This revolution in metaphysics proved disastrous for the political economy of Renaissance Florence and the early Dutch Republic. It also served Liberal modernity as an unquestioned ground.

Lastly, in chapter 4 I mobilize the aforementioned arguments to lay bare and repair the modern aesthetic project. At the outset, I assert the aesthetic is a symptom of the Liberal money form, not an antidote to it. Although construed expressly against the money relation, the aesthetic in fact mirrors Liberal money's impoverished metaphysics of haecceity. In so doing, the aesthetic naturalizes haecceity's contiguous here and now as the ultimate horizon of care. Offering a critique of modernity's gravitropic visuality, I make plain the limits of the aesthetic project and its surrender of care. Born with perspectival painting during the Florentine Renaissance, modernity's gravitropic visuality represses the abstract qualities of inscription and reduces the totality of being to a universally enjoyed gravity. Prefigured by Renaissance perspective, haecceity ferociously returns in neoliberal action-adventure media. Typified by the hyper-Newtonian blockbuster, this return reifies a false phenomenology of globalization. It also announces the historical exhaustion of the aesthetic project as such. Therefore, I conclude the book with an exhortation to divest gravitropism and pursue a radical reorganization of money's limitless locus of care.

My hope is that the book incites a host of previously repressed questions and concerns. For one, the sweeping arguments set forth here demand more extensive and fine-grained analyses. Isomorphism among Thomist metaphysics, legal writings, and Gothic abstraction suggest, for instance, a late medieval society struggling to make sense of the growing role of money in mediating collective existence. Yet the degree to which this society acknowledged, denied, or contested such isomorphism remains an open question. Artifacts from the period must be reexamined and the historiography of the late Middle Ages reconceived. Art historian Aden Kumler has noted, in this regard how, around 1075, the Eucharist wafer took the shape of a coin.[1] This occurred, meanwhile, as money relations grew in Western Christendom and church tithes were increasingly paid in coin. Kumler makes little of this, however, since she, like most scholars, reduces money to an unstable exchange relation and sovereignty to a problem of power. Approached from a neochartalist perspective, the convergence of icon and token provokes a number of questions. How deeply did such convergences penetrate late medieval consciousness? How might other artifacts make sense of and possibly complicate these meetings? Above all, how can late medieval culture assist us in imagining a new relationship to money?

Gravitropic visuality, too, requires additional consideration. An archive of collective longing for care, spectacular action changes form and meaning from context to context. The movements of Baroque painting are nothing like the postures of

Neoclassicism, and both Baroque and Neoclassical action differ from the ethereal leaps and bounds of early cinema. George Lucas and Steven Spielberg share interests, meanwhile, with postminimalist artists, including those like Robert Morris who pursue material presence and irregular process. Gravitropic visuality affects nonvisual media, too, from the hyperarticulated immediacy of Renaissance prose to the swirling immersiveness of digital surround sound. In all, these distinctions and correspondences constitute seeds for a new history of modern money, one that transcends the haecceity to which contemporary historiographies are uncritically attached.

Transcending haecceity proves equally important for theorists of technology and media, who typically presume money is profoundly shaped by shifting technical regimes. Hardly wrong for linking technological to sociopolitical change, these thinkers nonetheless ascribe *too much* transformative potential to technological advances and *too little* causal efficacy to monetary governance. Take digital and networking technologies, which have hastened enormous and often asymmetrical changes in political economic structures. Amplifying the scale and pace of collective life, they seem to globalize and accelerate social mediation processes. Overlooked by technology and media theorists, however, are the limited effects that algorithms and packet switching have had on money's underlying structures, capacities, and operations. Neglected, too, is the greater role played by fiscal policy and law in structuring global mediation, as much as the social and political meaning of technology. If, therefore, the field is to discern the significance of mediation processes, then it must explore how a centralized and inalienable money relation conditions them from the start.

Finally, *Declarations of Dependence* presents challenges to ecocriticism, New Materialism, and Speculative Realism. Concerned with ecological relationality, processes of materialization, and the primacy of the real, respectively, these fields tend to hold different and even competing views. Still, they share an interest in radically decentering critical theory. Positing a nonanthropocentric and underdetermined macrocosm that engulfs and structures a human-centered world, ecocriticism, New Materialism, and Speculative Realism variously theorize the aesthetic, ethical, and political consequences of this ontological commitment. A welcome corrective to the human hubris responsible for economic and ecological violence, these theories nevertheless naturalize the decentered haecceity I critique here. Disregarding money's mediation of human and nonhuman relations, these theories also amplify the phenomenology of Liberal modernity by anchoring matter and meaning in a mobile thisness. The result hinders any transformation of the human-nonhuman interface. One does better to ground this encounter in the resolutely centralized public instrument through which all human activity passes.

Above all, I wish this book to inspire new questions and counterintuitive theses that follow MMT's lines of sight and thought. To this end, I offer the following: To what extent is *capitalism* an adequate name for the social totality that modern money conditions? Deriving from the words *capital* and *capitalist*, the signifier *capitalism* emerged in the late nineteenth century as a largely critical term for a political economy perceived as private investment and exchange.[2] Yet this is precisely the problem. Hinging monetary relations on private actors and decentered market forces, the name capitalism obscures money's political topology and social capacities. The blind spot widens, moreover, when we project this vision onto the history of modern money and imagine bankers and merchants as prime movers of modernity. For this reason, I have avoided direct references to capitalism in *Declarations of Dependence*, a challenge I proffer to critical theory more generally.

Let us invent a post-Liberal language that makes money's boundless center feel, as Josef Albers remarked of abstraction, "more real than nature."[3] Let us then mobilize our finite resources to mend the vulnerable planet to which we have laid waste. This endeavor must be at once collective and contested, daring and continuous. Through such an effort, the provocations ventured here will become second nature, enabling the real work of politics to begin.

NOTES

INTRODUCTION

1. Jerry Ibbotson, "*Spectre*: A Brilliant Bond for the Age of Austerity," *YorkMix*, November 15, 2105, accessed June 30, 2016, http://www .yorkmix.com/things- to-do/films/film-review-spectre-brilliant -bond-for-the-age-of-austerity/.

2. L. Randall Wray, *Understanding Modern Money: The Key to Full Employment and Price Stability* (Northampton MA: Edward Elgar Publishing, 2006).

3. Scott Fullwiler, "Interest Rates and Fiscal Sustainability," Working Paper no. 53, Levy Economics Institute of Bard College (July 2006), accessed August 1, 2016, http://www.cfeps.org/pubs/wp-pdf/wp53 -Fullwiler.pdf, 15.

4. L. Randall Wray, "Policy for Full Employment and Price Stability," in *Modern Money Theory: A Primer on Macroeconomics for Sovereign Monetary Systems* (New York: Palgrave Macmillan, 2012), 221–60.

5. Karl Marx, *Capital, Volume One: A Critique of Political Economy* (New York: Dover Publications, 2011), 125.

6. Terry Eagleton, *The Ideology of the Aesthetic* (Oxford: Blackwell Publishers, 1991).

7. Thomas Schatz, "The New Hollywood," in *Film Theory Goes to the Movies*, ed. Jim Collins, Hilary Radner, and Ava Preacher Collins (New York: Routledge, 1993), 8–37.

8. David Bordwell, Janet Staiger, and Kristin Thompson, *The Classical Hollywood Cinema: Film Style and Mode of Production to 1960* (New York: Columbia University Press, 1985).

9. Frederick Wasser, *Steven Spielberg's America* (New York: Polity, 2010), 66.

10. Alexander Galloway, *Gaming: Essays on Algorithmic Culture* (Minneapolis: University of Minnesota Press, 2006), 39–69.

11. Amy Rust, *Passionate Detachments: Technologies of Vision and Violence in American Cinema, 1967–1974* (New York: SUNY Press, 2017).

12. Chester McArthur Destler, *American Radicalism: 1865–1901* (Chicago: Quadrangle Books, 1946).

13. Hilton Kramer, "Abstraction and Utopia," in *The Triumph of Modernism: The Art World, 1985–2005* (New York: Rowan & Littlefield, 2009), 34.

14. Theodor W. Adorno, *Aesthetic Theory*, trans. Robert Hulot-Kentor (London: Bloomsbury, 2013), 29–30.

15. Fredric Jameson, *Postmodernism, or, The Cultural Logic of Late Capitalism* (Durham NC: Duke University Press, 1997), 6.

16. Ernst H. Kantorowicz, *The King's Two Bodies: A Study in Medieval Political Theology* (Princeton NJ: Princeton University Press, 1997), 87–192.

17. Hans Baron, *The Crisis of the Early Italian Renaissance: Civic Humanism and Republican Liberty in an Age of Classicism and Tyranny* (Princeton NJ: Princeton University Press, 1966).

18. David S. Peterson, "The War of the Eight Saints," in *Society and Individual in Renaissance Florence*, ed. by William J. Connell (Berkeley: University of California Press, 2002), 173–214.

19. Lorenzo Valla, ed., and trans. Brendan Cook, *Correspondence* (Cambridge MA: Harvard University Press, 2013), 111. I am indebted to Cook for this alternative translation.

20. René Descartes, *Meditations on First Philosophy with Selections from the Objections and Replies*, trans. and ed. John Cottingham (Cambridge: Cambridge University Press, 1996), 16–23.

21. John Locke, *An Essay Concerning Human Understanding: Complete and Unabridged in One Volume* (Greensborough NC: WLC, 2009).

22. Adam Smith, "The History of Astronomy," in *The Essential Adam Smith*, ed. Robert L. Heilbroner (New York: W. W. Norton & Company, 1987), 22–37.

23. Adam Smith, *An Inquiry into the Nature and Causes of the Wealth of Nations*, ed. R. H. Campbell, A. S. Skinner, and W. B. Todd (Oxford: Oxford University Press, 1976).

24. See David Hume, *A Treatise of Human Nature: Being an Attempt to Introduce the Experimental Method of Reasoning into Moral Subjects* (New York: Penguin Classics, 1986).

25. David Hume, *Political Discourses (1752)* (Whitefish MT: Kessinger Publishing, 2009).

26. Marx, *Capital, Volume One*, 103–4.

27. Marx, *Capital, Volume One*, 81–161.

28. Marx, *Capital, Volume One*, 125.

29. Marx, *Capital, Volume One*, 257; Mark Neocleous, "The Political Economy of the Dead: Marx's Vampires," *History of Political Thought* 24, no. 4 (Winter 2003): 668–84.

30. Karl Marx, *The Economic and Philosophic Manuscripts of 1844*. See *The Economic and Philosophic Manuscripts of 1844 and the Communist Manifesto*, trans. Martin Milligan (Amherst MA: Prometheus Books, 1988), 138. Later Marx speaks of money's "monstrous exactions," in *Capital, Volume One*, 268.

31. Marshall Berman, *All That Is Solid Melts into Air: The Experience of Modernity* (New York: Penguin Books, 1988), 19.

32. Karl Marx and Friedrich Engels, *Manifesto of the Communist Party*, trans. Samuel Moore (Radford VA: Wilder Publications, 2008), 11; Berman, *All That Is Solid Melts into Air*, 19.

33. Max Horkheimer, *Critical Theory: Selected Essays* (London: Continuum Publishing, 1975), 219–20.

34. Yanis Varoufakis, *The Global Minotaur: America, Europe and the Future of the Global Economy* (London: Zed Books, 2013), 64–65.

35. L. Randall Wray, "Teoría Monetaria Moderna ¿Austeridad presupuestaria frente a déficits públicos?", delivered at Open Space FUHEM, Saturday, March 7, 2015, http://www.fuhem.es/ecosocial/noticias.aspx?v=9715&n=0.

1. TRANSCENDING THE AESTHETIC

1. Peter Bürger, *Theory of the Avant-Garde*, trans. Michael Shaw (Minneapolis: University of Minnesota Press, 1984), 50.

2. McKenzie Wark, *Telesthesia: Communication, Culture & Class* (Cambridge: Polity, 2012), 34.

3. Nicholas Brown, "The Work of Art in the Age of Its Real Subsumption under Capital," *Nonsite.org*, March 13, 2012, http://nonsite

.org/editorial/the-work-of-art-in-the-age-of-its-real-subsumption
-under-capital.

4. Sven Lütticken, "The Coming Exception: Art and the Crisis of Value," *New Left Review* 99 (May–June 2016): 113.

5. Christine Desan, "Creation Stories," in *Making Money: Coin, Bank Currency, and the Coming of Capitalism* (Oxford: Oxford University Press, 2014), 23–69.

6. Adam Smith, *An Inquiry into the Nature and Causes of the Wealth of Nations*, ed. R. H. Campbell, A. S. Skinner, and W. B. Todd (Oxford: Oxford University Press, 1976), 25.

7. Niall Ferguson, *The Ascent of Money: A Financial History of the World* (New York: Penguin Books, 2009), 17–64; Paul Krugman, "There's Something about Money (Implicitly Wonkish)," The Conscience of a Liberal, *New York Times*, February 10, 2015, accessed September 8, 2016, http://krugman.blogs.nytimes.com/2015/02/10/theres-something-about-money-implicitly-wonkish/?_r=0; Nigel Dodd, Interview with Craig Barfoot, "The Social Life of Money," Pod Academy, February 1, 2015, http://podacademy.org/podcasts/social-life-money/.

8. Karl Marx, *Theories of Surplus Value* (Amherst MA: Prometheus Books, 2000).

9. Karl Marx, *Capital, Volume One, 255–56*, quoted in Moishe Postone, *Time, Labor, and Social Domination: A Reinterpretation of Marx's Critical Theory* (Cambridge: Cambridge University Press, 1995), 75.

10. Karl Marx, *Capital, Volume One: A Critique of Political Economy* (New York: Dover Publications, 2011), 123.

11. Karl Marx, *Grundrisse: Foundations of the Critique of Political Economy*, trans. Martin Nicolaus (New York: Penguin Books, 1973), 745–52.

12. Karl Marx, *Capital: A Critique of Political Economy, Volume Three* (New York: Penguin Classics, 1993), 525–42.

13. Carl Menger, "On the Origins of Money," *Economic Journal* 2 (1892): 239–55.

14. Friedrich Engels, *The Condition of the Working Class in England*, trans. David McLellan (Oxford: Oxford University Press, 2009), 96.

15. Judith Stein, *Pivotal Decade: How the United States Traded Factories for Finance in the Seventies* (New Haven CT: Yale University Press, 2010), 113, 225–37.

16. Rebecca L. Spang, *Money and Stuff in the Time of the French Revolution* (Cambridge: Harvard University Press, 2015); Leon Trotsky, *The History of the Russian Revolution*, trans. Max Eastman (London: Pluto Press, 1977), 422–25; Dmitri Volkogonov, *Lenin: A New Biography*, trans. Harold Shukman (New York: Free Press, 1994), 338–39.

17. Diedrich Diederichsen, *On (Surplus) Value in Art: Reflections 01* (Berlin: Sternberg Press, 2008), 23.

18. Martin Jay, *Cultural Semantics: Keywords of Our Times* (Cambridge: University of Massachusetts Press, 2012); Jacques Rancière, *Aesthetics and Its Discontents*, trans. Steven Corcoran (Cambridge: Polity Press, 2009); Nicholas Brown, "The Work of Art in the Age of Its Real Subsumption under Capital," *Nonsite.org* (March 2013), accessed April 5, 2017, http://nonsite.org/editorial/the-work-of-art-in-the-age-of-its-real-subsumption-under-capital; Lisa Siraganian, *Modernism's Other Work: The Art Object's Political Life* (Oxford: Oxford University Press, 2012); Dave Beech, *Art and Value: Art's Economic Exceptionalism in Classical, Neoclassical and Marxist Economics* (Leiden, Netherlands: Brill, 2015).

19. Theodor W. Adorno, *Aesthetic Theory*, trans. Robert Hullot-Kentor (London: Bloomsbury, 2013); Peter Bürger, *Theory of the Avant-Garde*, trans. Michael Shaw (Minneapolis: University of Minnesota Press, 1984); Pierre Bourdieu, *The Rules of Art: Genesis and Structure of the Literary Field*, trans. Susan Emanuel (Stanford: Stanford University Press, 1996).

20. Patrick Jagoda, N. Katherine Hayles, and Patrick LeMieux, "Speculation: Financial Games and Derivative Worlding in a Transmedia Era," *Critical Inquiry* 40, no. 3 (Spring 2014): 220–36; Max Haiven, "Art and Money: Three Aesthetic Strategies in an Age of Financialisation," *Finance and Society* 1, no. 1 (2015): 38–60.

21. Fredric Jameson, *Postmodernism, or, The Cultural Logic of Late Capitalism* (Durham NC: Duke University Press, 1992); Yates McKee, "Occupy and the End of Socially Engaged Art," *e-flux* 72 (April 2016), http://www.e-flux.com/journal/occupy- and-the-end-of-socially-engaged-art-an-historical-snapshot/#_ftnref13; Monika Szewczyk, "Exchange and Some Change: The Imaginative Economies of Otobong Nkanga," *Afterall* 37 (Autumn–Winter 2014): 38–51.

22. Brett Scott, *The Heretic's Guide to Global Finance: Hacking the Future of Money* (London: Pluto Press, 2013); Rob Myers, "(Conceptual) Art, Cryptocurrency and Beyond," *Furtherfield* (October 2014), accessed September 8, 2016, http://furtherfield.org/features/articles/conceptual-art-cryptocurrency- and-beyond; Alex Williams and Nick Srnicek, "#ACCELERATE MANIFESTO for an Accelerationist Politics," *Critical Legal Thinking*, May 14, 2013, accessed September 8, 2016, http://criticallegalthinking.com/2013/05/14/accelerate-manifesto-for-an-accelerationist-politics/; Joshua Clover, *Red Epic* (Berkeley, CA: Commune Editions, 2015).

23. John Howkins, *The Creative Economy: How People Make Money from Ideas* (New York: Penguin, 2002).

24. Claire Fontaine, "Our Common Critical Condition," trans. Kit Schluter, *e-flux* 73 (May 2016), http://www.e-flux.com/journal/our-common-critical-condition/.

25. Theodor Adorno, *Minima Moralia: Reflections on a Damaged Life*, trans. E. F. N. Jephcott (London: Verso, 2006).

26. Thomas Tooke, *An Inquiry into the Currency Principle: The Connection of the Currency with Prices, and the Expediency of a Separation of Issue from Banking* (London: Forgotten Books, 2015); John Fullarton, *On the Regulation of Currencies* (London: Forgotten Books, 2012); Edward Kellogg, *Labor and Other Capital* (New York: A. M. Kelley, 1978).

27. Georg Friedrich Knapp, *The State Theory of Money*, trans. J. Bonar and H. M. Lucas (New York: Simon Publications, 2003), 1.

28. Alfred Mitchell Innes, *Credit and State Theories of Money: The Contributions of A. Mitchell Innes*, ed. L. Randall Wray (Northampton MA: Edward Elgar Publishing, 2004).

29. Geoffrey Ingham, "Babylonian Madness: On the Historical and Sociological Origins of Money," in *What Is Money?*, ed. John Smithin (London: Routledge, 2000), 16–41.

30. John Maynard Keynes, *A Treatise on Money* (London: Macmillan, 1930), 4–5.

31. John Maynard Keynes, *The General Theory of Employment, Interest and Money* (New York: Harcourt-Brace & World, 1936).

32. Michal Kalecki, *Collected Works of Michal Kalecki (Seven Volumes)* (Oxford: Oxford University Press, 1990); Hyman Minsky, *Stabilizing*

an *Unstable Economy* (New York: McGraw Hill, 2008); Abba P. Lerner, *The Economics of Control* (London: Macmillan, 1944).

33. Michal Kalecki, "The Political Aspects of Full Employment," in *The Economics of Full Employment: Six Studies in Applied Economics Prepared at the Oxford University Institute of Statistics* (Oxford: Blackwell, 1943).

34. Hyman Minsky, *Ending Poverty: Jobs, Not Welfare* (Annandale-on-Hudson NY: Levy Economics Institute, 2013).

35. Abba P. Lerner, "Functional Finance and the Federal Debt," in *Readings in Fiscal Policy* (Homewood AL: Richard D. Irwin, 1955), 469.

36. David Colander, "Was Keynes a Keynesian or a Lernerian?" *Journal of Economic Literature* 22, no. 4 (1984): 1574.

37. Colander, "Was Keynes a Keynesian," 1574.

38. Colander, "Was Keynes a Keynesian," 1574.

39. Colander, "Was Keynes a Keynesian," 1574.

40. Marc Lavoie, "A Primer on Endogenous Credit-Money," in *Modern Theories of Money: The Nature and Role of Money in Capitalist Economies*, ed. Louis-Philippe Rochon and Sergio Rossi (Northampton MA: Edward Elgar Publishing, 2003): 506–43.

41. L. Randall Wray, "Modern Money Theory: Intellectual Origins and Policy Implications," International and Comparative Law Center (ICLC) Seminar Series, October 2015, accessed September 6, 2016, https://www.youtube.com/watch?v=-kri9nf8biA.

42. Warren Mosler, "Soft Currency Economics," *The Center of the Universe*, February 1995, accessed September 30, 2016, http://moslereconomics.com/mandatory-readings/soft-currency-economics/.

43. Mosler, "Soft Currency Economics."

44. Warren Mosler and Mathew Forstater, "The Natural Rate of Interest is Zero," *Journal of Economic Issues* 39, no. 2 (June 2005): 535–42.

45. Warren Mosler, *The Seven Deadly Innocent Frauds of Economic Policy* (St. Croix, U.S. Virgin Islands: Valance Company, 2010), 18.

46. L. Randall Wray, "When Will They Ever Learn—Uncle Sam Is Not Robin Hood," *Naked Capitalism*, March 5, 2014, accessed September 12, 2016, http://www.nakedcapitalism.com/2014/03/randy-wray-will-ever-learn-uncle-sam-robin-hood.html.

47. L. Randall Wray, "Teoría Monetaria Moderna ¿Austeridad presupuestaria frente a déficits públicos?," delivered at Open Space

FUHEM, Saturday, March 7, 2015, http://www.fuhem.es/ecosocial
/noticias.aspx?v=9715&n=0.

48. L. Randall Wray, "The Value of Redemption (Debt Free Money,
Part 3)," *Naked Capitalism*, February 16, 2016, accessed September
8, 2016, http://www.nakedcapitalism.com/2016/02/randy-wray-the
-value-of-redemption-debt-free-money-part-3.html.

49. Marx, *Capital, Volume One*, 81.

2. DECLARATIONS OF DEPENDENCE

1. Michel Foucault, *Security, Territory, Population: Lectures at the Collège de
France, 1977–1978*, trans. Graham Burchell (New York: Palgrave Macmil-
lan, 2007); Michel Foucault, *Society Must Be Defended*, ed. Mauro Bertani
and Allesandro Fontana, trans. David Macey (New York: Picador, 2003);
Michel Foucault, *The Government of the Self and Others*, ed. Frédéric
Gros, trans. Graham Burchell (New York: Palgrave Macmillan, 2010).

2. Theodor Adorno, *Minima Moralia: Reflections from Damaged Life*,
trans. E. F. N. Jephcott (London: Verso, 2006), 22–23.

3. Karl Marx, *Capital, Volume One: A Critique of Political Economy* (New
York: Dover Publications, 2011), 784–865.

4. Max Weber, *Weber's Rationalism and Modern Society*, trans. and ed. Tony
Waters and Dagmar Waters (London: Palgrave Books, 2015), 129–98.

5. L. Randall Wray, *Understanding Modern Money: The Key to Full Employment and Price Stability* (Northampton MA: Edward Elgar Publishing,
2006), 47–51; Warren Mosler, *The Seven Deadly Innocent Frauds of
Economic Policy* (St. Croix, U.S. Virgin Islands: Valance Company,
2010), 18–20.

6. John Harvey, "The Social Origins of Money: The Case of Egypt," in
Credit and State Theories of Money: The Contributions of A. Mitchell Innes,
ed. L. Randall Wray (Northampton MA: Edward Elgar, 2004), 70–98.

7. Christine Desan, *Making Money: Coin, Currency, and the Coming of
Capitalism* (Oxford: Oxford University Press, 2014), 7.

8. Desan, *Making Money*, 7.

9. Desan, *Making Money*, 7.

10. Geoffrey Ingham, *The Nature of Money* (Cambridge: Polity, 2004), 4.

11. Quoted in Heidegger, *Being and Time*, trans. John Macquarrie and
Edward Robinson (New York: Harper Perennial Modern Classics,
2008), 242.

12. Warrant T. Reich, *Encyclopedia of Bioethics*, revised edition, ed. Warren Thomas Reich, 5 vols. (New York: Simon & Schuster Macmillan, 1995), 319–31.

13. Jean Graybeal, *Language and "The Feminine" in Nietzsche and Heidegger* (Bloomington: Indiana University Press, 1990), 126; Katrin Froese, *Nietzsche, Heidegger and Daoist Thought: Crossing Paths In-Between* (Albany: SUNY Press, 2007), 188.

14. Fredric Jameson, "The Vanishing Mediator: Narrative Structure in Max Weber," *New German Critique* 1 (Winter 1973): 52–89.

15. Martin Heidegger, "What Are Poets For?," *Poetry, Language, Thought*, ed. J. Glenn Gray, trans. Albert Hofstadter (New York: Harper & Row Publishers, 1971), 104.

16. Heidegger, *Being and Time*, 34.

17. Heidegger, "What Are Poets For?," 107.

18. Heidegger, "What Are Poets For?," 104.

19. Heidegger, "What Are Poets For?," 104.

20. Heidegger, "What Are Poets For?," 120.

21. Heidegger, ". . . Poetically, Man Dwells . . . ," *Poetry, Language, Thought*, 226.

22. Heidegger, "What Are Poets For?," 113.

23. Heidegger, "What Are Poets For?," 114–15.

24. Heidegger, "What Are Poets For?," 135.

25. Heidegger, "Language," *Poetry, Language, Thought*, 201–2.

26. Judith Butler, *Subjects of Desire: Hegelian Reflections in Twentieth-Century France* (New York: Columbia University Press, 1999); *Gender Trouble: Feminism and the Subversion of Identity* (London: Routledge, 2006).

27. Friedrich Nietzsche, *On the Genealogy of Morals*, trans. Douglas Smith (Oxford: Oxford University Press, 2009).

28. Judith Butler, "On Cruelty," *London Review of Books* 36, no. 14 (July 17, 2014).

29. Butler, "On Cruelty," 31.

30. Butler, "On Cruelty," 32.

31. Butler, "On Cruelty," 32.

32. Butler, "On Cruelty," 32.

33. Butler, "On Cruelty," 32–33.

34. Butler, "On Cruelty," 33.

35. Butler, "On Cruelty," 33.

36. Judith Butler, *Notes Toward a Performative Theory of Assembly* (Cambridge: Harvard University Press, 2015), 21.

37. Butler, *Notes Toward a Performative Theory of Assembly*, 96.

38. Butler, *Notes Toward a Performative Theory of Assembly*, 11.

39. Judith Butler, "Bodies in Alliance and the Politics of the Street," Transversal Texts, European Institute for Progressive Cultural Policies, September, 2011, accessed September 24, 2016, http://www.eipcp.net/transversal/1011/butler/en.

40. Butler, "On Cruelty," 32.

41. Rania Antonopoulos, "The *Right* to a Job, The *Right Types* of Projects: Employment Guarantee Policies from a Gender Perspective," Working Paper no. 516, Levy Economics Institute of Bard College, September 2007, accessed September 28, 2106, http://www.levyinstitute.org/pubs/wp_516.pdf; Nancy Fraser, "Behind Marx's Hidden Abode: For An Expanded Conception of Capitalism," *New Left Review* 86 (March 2014): 55; Mathew Forstater, "Green Jobs: Addressing the Critical Issues Surrounding the Environment, Workplace and Employment," *International Journal of Environment, Workplace and Employment* 1, no. 1 (2004): 53–61; Michael Hoexter, "Effective Climate Action Is a Building Project," *New Economic Perspectives*, October 2, 2014, accessed September 28, 2016, http://neweconomicperspectives.org/2014/10/effective-climate-action-building-project.html; Modern Money Network, "Free Culture? Free Finance," *Morningside Muckraker,* October 28, 2014, accessed September 28, 2106, http://morningsidemuckraker.com/free-culture-free-finance/.

42. Pavlina R. Tcherneva, "Permanent On-the-Spot Job Creation—The Missing Keynes Plan for Full Employment and Economic Transformation," *Review of Social Economy* 70, no. 1 (2012): 57–80; "Employer of Last Resort," in *The Elgar Companion to Post Keynesian Economics,* ed. J. E. King (Northampton MA: Edward Elgar, 2012), 161–65.

43. Andrea Liss, "Maternal Care: Mierle Laderman Ukeles's Maintenance Art," *Feminist Art and the Maternal* (Minneapolis: University of Minnesota Press, 2009), 43–67; Shannon Jackson, "High Maintenance: The Sanitation Aesthetics of Mierle Laderman Ukeles," in

Social Works: Supporting Art, Performing Publics (London: Routledge, 2011), 75–103.

44. Quoted in Lucy Lippard, *Six Years: The Dematerialization of the Art Object* (New York: New York University Press, 1979), *Six Years*, 220.

45. Quoted in Lippard, *Six Years*, 220.

46. Quoted in Lippard, *Six Years*, 220.

47. Quoted in Lippard, *Six Years*, 220.

48. Quoted in Lippard, *Six Years*, 220.

49. Quoted in Lippard, *Six Years*, 220.

50. Holland Cotter, "An Artist Redefines Power. With Sanitation Equipment," *New York Times*, September 15, 2016, accessed September 27, 2016, http://www.nytimes.com/2016/09/16/arts/design/an-artist-redefines-power-with-sanitation-equipment.html.

51. D. W. Winnicott, *Playing and Reality* (London: Routledge, 1982).

52. Esther Bick, "The Experience of the Skin in Early Object-Relations," *International Journal of Psychoanalysis* 49, no. 2–3 (1968): 484–86; Thomas H. Ogden, *The Primitive Edge of Experience* (London: Aronson, 1989).

53. D. W. Winnicott, "The Theory of the Parent-Infant Relation," *International Journal of Psychoanalysis* 41 (1960): 585–95, 590.

54. Fredric Jameson, *Postmodernism, or, The Cultural Logic of Late Capitalism* (Durham NC: Duke University Press, 1992), 52.

3. *MEDIUM CONGRUENTISSIMUM*

1. Steven Ozment, *The Age of Reform: 1250–1550: An Intellectual and Religious History of Late Medieval and Reformation Europe* (New Haven CT: Yale University Press, 1980), 2.

2. W. E. Lunt, "The Financial System of the Medieval Papacy in Light of Recent Literature," *Quarterly Journal of Economics* 23 no. 2 (February 1909): 251–95.

3. Lunt, "The Financial System," 251–52.

4. Gregory of Nyssa, "The Great Catechism," 37, in *A Select Library of Nicene and Post-Nicene Fathers of the Christian Church*, vol. 5: *Gregory of Nyssa*, trans. Philip Schaff and Henry Wace (New York: Christian Literature Company, 1893), 505.

5. Gary Macy, "Introduction," in *A Companion to the Eucharist in the Middle Ages*, ed. Ian Levy, Gary Macy, and Kristen Van Ausdall (Leiden, Netherlands: Brill, 2011), 3.

6. Charles Redding and Francis Newton, *Theology, Rhetoric, and Politics in the Eucharistic Controversy, 1078–1079* (New York: Columbia University Press, 2003), 10.

7. Eamon Duffy, *The Stripping of the Altars, c. 1450–c. 1580* (New Haven CT: Yale University Press, 1992), 91–92.

8. Duffy, *The Stripping of the Altars*, 112.

9. Duffy, *The Stripping of the Altars*, 111.

10. Cited in Ozment, *The Age of Reform*, 52–53.

11. Robert Pasnau, "Abstract Truth in Thomas Aquinas," in *Representation and Objects of Thought in Medieval Philosophy*, ed. Henrik Lagerlund (Burlington VT: Ashgate Publishing, 1997), 33–62.

12. Thomas Aquinas, *Summa Contra Gentiles Book 4: Salvation*, ed. Charles J. O'Neil (Notre Dame IN: University of Notre Dame Press, 1975), lib. 4, cap. 64, n. 4.

13. Aquinas, *Summa Theologica*, III^a q. 75 a. 1 ad 3.

14. Brian Davies, *Thomas Aquinas's Summa Theologiae: A Guide and Commentary* (Oxford: Oxford University Press, 2014), 329.

15. Aquinas, *Summa Theologica* III^a q. 75 a. 2 co.

16. Friedrich Nietzsche, "On Truth or Lie in an Extramoral Sense," in *The Continental Aesthetics Reader*, ed. Clive Cazeaux (London: Routledge, 2011), 71.

17. Ernst Kantorowicz, *The King's Two Bodies: A Study in Medieval Political Theology* (Princeton: Princeton University Press, 1997), 186.

18. Kantorowicz, *The King's Two Bodies*, 184.

19. Kantorowicz, *The King's Two Bodies*, 168.

20. Kantorowicz, *The King's Two Bodies*, 201, 202, 201.

21. Kantorowicz, *The King's Two Bodies*, 184, 186, 185.

22. Kantorowicz, *The King's Two Bodies*, 184, 177, 189.

23. Kantorowicz, *The King's Two Bodies*, 184.

24. Kantorowicz, *The King's Two Bodies*, 173.

25. Kantorowicz, *The King's Two Bodies*, 173.

26. Marylin McCord Adams, *Some Later Medieval Theories of the Eucharist: Thomas Aquinas, Giles of Rome, Duns Scotus, and William of Ockham* (Oxford: Oxford University Press, 2010), 154.

27. David S. Peterson, "The War of the Eight Saints," in *Society and Individual in Renaissance Florence*, ed. William J. Connell (Berkeley: University of California Press, 2002), 182.

28. Ozment, *The Age of Reform*, 61–62.

29. Nicholas de Cusa, *Selected Spiritual Writings*, trans. H. Lawrence Bond (Costa Mesa CA: Paulist Press, 2005), 158, 161.

30. Richard A. Goldthwaite, *The Economy of Renaissance Florence* (Baltimore MA: Johns Hopkins University Press, 2009); Samuel Kline Cohn Jr., *The Laboring Classes in Renaissance Florence* (New York: Academic Press, 1980); Gene A. Brucker, *Florentine Politics and Society, 1343–1378* (Princeton NJ: Princeton University Press, 1962).

31. Donald E. Brown, *Hierarchy, History, and Human Nature: The Social Origins of Historical Consciousness* (Tucson: University of Arizona Press, 1988), 269.

32. Anthony Molho, *Florentine Public Finances in the Early Renaissance, 1400–1433* (Cambridge MA: Harvard University Press, 1971), 20.

33. David Herlihy, *Medieval and Renaissance Pistoia: The Social History of an Italian Town, 1200–1430* (New Haven CT: Yale University Press, 1967), 191.

34. Peterson, "The War of the Eight Saints," 198.

35. Peterson, "The War of the Eight Saints," 205–6.

36. Peterson, "The War of the Eight Saints," 204–5.

37. Ronald G. Witt, *In the Footsteps of the Ancients: The Origins of Humanism from Lovato to Bruni* (Leiden, Netherlands: Brill, 2000).

38. Lorenzo Valla, *Correspondence*, trans. Brendan Cook (Cambridge: Harvard University Press), 83.

39. Poggio Bracciolini, *De avaritia*, ed. Giuseppe Germano (Livorno, Italy: Belforte, 1994).

40. Christian Bec, *Les Marchands Ecrivains à Florence, 1375–1434* (Paris: Mouton, 1967), 381. My translation.

41. Quoted in Margaret L. King, *The Renaissance in Europe* (London: Laurence King Publishing, 2003), 81.

42. Jared Poley, *The Devil's Riches: A Modern History of Greed* (New York: Berghahn Books, 2016), 21–22.

43. Juliann M. Vitullo and Diane Wolfthal, "Trading Values: Negotiating Masculinity in Late Medieval and Early Modern Europe," in *Money, Morality, and Culture in Late Medieval and Early Modern Europe*,

ed. Juliann M. Vitullo and Diane Wolfthal (Furnham, England: Ashgate Publishing, 2010), 157.

44. Desiderius Erasmus, *Collected Works of Spiritualia, Volume 66*, trans. John W. O'Malley (Toronto: University of Toronto Press, 1988), 141.

45. Michelangelo Buonarroti, *The Sonnets of Michelangelo*, trans. Elizabeth Jennings (London: Folio Society, 1961), 24.

46. Marjorie O'Rourke Boyle, *Petrarch's Genius: Pentimento and Prophecy* (Berkeley: University of California Press, 1991), 142–43.

47. Buonarroti, *The Sonnets of Michelangelo*, 24.

48. Buonarroti, *The Sonnets of Michelangelo*, 24.

49. Buonarroti, *The Sonnets of Michelangelo*, 24.

4. ALLEGORIES OF THE AESTHETIC

1. Geoffrey Galt Harpham, *Shadows of Ethics: Criticism and the Just Society* (Durham NC: Duke University Press, 1999), 120.

2. Harpham, *Shadows of Ethics*, 120.

3. Pamela R. Matthew and David McWhirter, introduction to *Aesthetic Subjects*, ed. Pamela R. Matthew and David McWhirter (Minneapolis: University of Minnesota Press: 2003), xiv.

4. Theodor W. Adorno, *Negative Dialectics*, trans. E. B. Ashton (London: Bloomsbury, 1981), 17–18.

5. Alexandre Koyre, *A Documentary History of the Problem of Fall from Kepler to Newton: De Motu Gravium Naturaliter Cadentium in Hypothesi Terrae Motae* (Whitefish MT: Literary Licensing, 2012).

6. Ezio Vailati, *Leibniz and Clarke: A Study of their Correspondence* (Oxford: Oxford University Press, 1997), 186.

7. Immanuel Kant, *Metaphysical Foundations of Natural Science*, trans. and ed. Michael Freeman (Cambridge: Cambridge University Press, 2004); Friedrich Schelling, *The Ages of the World*, trans. Jason W. Wirth (New York: SUNY Press, 2000), 92, 107; Friedrich Nietzsche, "The Spirit of Gravity," in *Thus Spoke Zarathustra*, trans. and ed. Stanley Applebaum (Mineola NY: Dover, 2004), 133–36.

8. Michael Baxandall, *Giotto and the Orators: Humanist Observers of Painting in Italy and the Discovery of Pictorial Composition, 1350–1450* (Oxford: Clarendon Press, 1971).

9. Baxandall, *Giotto and the Orators*, 63–64.

10. Baxandall, *Giotto and the Orators*, 131.

11. Baxandall, *Giotto and the Orators*, 137.

12. Baxandall, *Giotto and the Orators*, 130–39.

13. Charles Sanders Peirce, *Essential Peirce: Selected Philosophical Writings, 1893–1913*, vol. 2, ed. Peirce Edition Project (Bloomington: Indiana University Press, 1998), 9.

14. Steven Ozment, *The Age of Reform, 1250—1550: An Intellectual and Religious History of Late Medieval and Reformation Europe* (New Haven CT: Yale University Press, 1980), 60.

15. Quoted in Giulio Carlo Argan and Nesca A. Robb, "The Architecture of Brunelleschi," *Journal of the Warburg and Courtauld Institutes* 9 (1946): 120.

16. Gene Brucker, *The Civic World of Early Renaissance Florence* (Princeton: Princeton University Press, 1977), 406.

17. David S. Peterson, "The War of the Eight Saints," in *Society and Individual in Renaissance Florence*, ed. William J. Connell (Berkeley: University of California Press, 2002), 212.

18. Isaac Newton, *Isaac Newton: Philosophical Writings*, ed. A. Janiak (Cambridge: Cambridge University Press, 2004), 21, 138.

19. Karl Marx, *The First Writings of Karl Marx*, ed. Paul M. Schafer (New York: Ig Publishing, 2006); Schelling, *The Ages of the World*.

20. Michael Friedman, "Newton and Kant on Absolute Space: From Theology to Transcendental Philosophy," in *Constituting Objectivity: Transcendental Perspectives on Modern Physics*, ed. Michel Bitbol, Pierre Kerszberg, and Jean Petito (New York: Springer, 2009), 49.

21. Friedman, "Newton and Kant on Absolute Space," 44.

22. Charles M. Jones, *The Scarlet Pumpernickel* (Burbank CA: Warner Brothers, 1950).

23. Alfred Hitchcock, *Vertigo* (Hollywood CA: Paramount, 1958).

24. Aniela Jaffé, *The Myth of Meaning in the Work of C. J. Jung*, trans. R. F. C. Hull (Zürich, Switzerland: Daimon Verlag, 1984), 66.

25. Christian Metz, *The Imaginary Signifier: Psychoanalysis and the Cinema*, trans. Celia Britton, Annwyll Williams, Ben Brewster, and Alfred Guzzetti (Bloomington: Indiana University Press, 1982), 54.

26. John Halas and Roger Manvell, *Design in Motion* (New York: Hastings House, 1962), 54–55.

27. Chuck Jones, *Duck Dodgers in the 24½th Century* (Burbank CA: Warner Brothers, 1953).

28. Jones, *Duck Dodgers in the 24½th Century*.

29. Leatrice Eiseman and Keith Recker, *Pantone: The 20th Century in Color* (San Francisco: Chronicle Books, 2011), 117.

30. Amy Rust, *Passionate Detachments: Technologies of Vision and Violence in American Cinema, 1967–1974* (New York: SUNY Press, 2017), 4.

31. Rust, *Passionate Detachments*, 3.

32. Judith Stein, *Pivotal Decade: How the United States Traded Factories for Finance in the Seventies* (New Haven CT: Yale University Press, 2010).

33. Bruce Schulman, *The Seventies: The Great Shift in American Culture, Society, and Politics* (New York: Free Press, 2001), 80.

34. Jefferson Cowie, *Stayin' Alive: The 1970s and the Last Days of the Working Class* (New York, 2010); Marisa Chappell, "Demanding a New Family Wage: Feminist Consensus in the 1970s Full Employment Campaign," in *Feminist Coalitions: Historical Perspectives on Second-Wave Feminism in the United States*, ed. Stephanie Gilmore (Champaign: University of Illinois Press, 2008), 252–84; David P. Stein, "Fearing Inflation, Inflating Fears: The End of Full Employment and the Rise of the Carceral State" (PhD diss., University of Southern California, 2014).

35. Scott Ferguson, "Towards Unbearable Lightness; or, Topsy-Turvy Technology in the New *Pooh*," *Screen* 55, no. 2 (Summer 2014):165–88.

36. Julie A. Turnock, *Plastic Reality: Special Effects, Technology, and the Emergence of 1970s Blockbuster Aesthetics* (New York: Columbia University Press, 2015), 23, 31.

37. Turnock, *Plastic Reality*, 60.

38. Turnock, *Plastic Reality*, 109.

39. George Lucas, *Star Wars: Episode IV—A New Hope* (Los Angeles CA: Twentieth Century Fox, 1977).

40. Lucas, *Star Wars: Episode IV—A New Hope*.

41. Turnock, *Plastic Reality*, 129.

42. Steven Spielberg, *Close Encounters of the Third Kind* (Culver City CA: Columbia Pictures, 1977).

43. Spielberg, *Close Encounters of the Third Kind*.

44. Kevin B. Lee, *Essential Viewing: The Spielberg Face*, video essay, 9.39 minutes, 2011, https://www.fandor.com/keyframe/essential-viewing -the-spielberg-face.

45. Don Hall and Chris Williams, *Big Hero 6* (Burbank CA: Disney, 2014).

46. Hall and Williams, *Big Hero 6*.
47. Hall and Williams, *Big Hero 6*.
48. Hall and Williams, *Big Hero 6*.

EPILOGUE

1. Aden Kumler, "The Multiplication of the Species: Eucharistic Morphology in the Middle Ages," RES: *Anthropology and Aesthetics* 59–60 (2011): 179–91.
2. Raymond Williams, *Keywords: A Vocabulary of Culture and Society* (New York: Oxford University Press, 1983), 50–52.
3. Katherine Kuh, *The Artist's Voice: Talks with Seventeen Modern Artists* (Boston: Da Capo Press, 2000), 11.

To order or obtain more information on these or other University of
Nebraska Press titles, visit nebraskapress.unl.edu.

CPSIA information can be obtained
at www.ICGtesting.com
Printed in the USA
LVHW08s1112180718
583945LV00008B/271/P

9 781496 201928